TRUST

THE

DOG

TRUST
THE
DOG

REBUILDING LIVES

THROUGH TEAMWORK

WITH MAN'S BEST FRIEND

The Fidelco Guide Dog Foundation

with Gerri Hirshey

VIKING

VIKING
Published by the Penguin Group
Penguin Group (USA) Inc., 375 Hudson Street, New York, New York 10014, U.S.A.
Penguin Group (Canada), 90 Eglinton Avenue East, Suite 700,
Toronto, Ontario, Canada M4P 2Y3
(a division of Pearson Penguin Canada Inc.)
Penguin Books Ltd, 80 Strand, London WC2R 0RL, England
Penguin Ireland, 25 St. Stephen's Green, Dublin 2, Ireland
(a division of Penguin Books Ltd)
Penguin Books Australia Ltd, 250 Camberwell Road, Camberwell, Victoria 3124, Australia
(a division of Pearson Australia Group Pty Ltd)
Penguin Books India Pvt Ltd, 11 Community Centre, Panchsheel Park,
New Delhi – 110 017, India
Penguin Group (NZ), 67 Apollo Drive, Rosedale, North Shore 0632, New Zealand
(a division of Pearson New Zealand Ltd)
Penguin Books (South Africa) (Pty) Ltd, 24 Sturdee Avenue, Rosebank,
Johannesburg 2196, South Africa

Penguin Books Ltd, Registered Offices: 80 Strand, London WC2R 0RL, England

First published in 2010 by Viking Penguin, a member of Penguin Group (USA) Inc.

1   3   5   7   9   10   8   6   4   2

Copyright © The Fidelco Guide Dog Foundation, Inc., 2010
All rights reserved

Photographs from The Fidelco Guide Dog Foundation unless otherwise indicated.

LIBRARY OF CONGRESS CATALOGING-IN-PUBLICATION DATA
Hirshey, Gerri.
Trust the dog : rebuilding lives through teamwork with man's best friend / The Fidelco Guide
Dog Foundation with Gerri Hirshey.
p. cm.
ISBN 978-0-670-02151-2
1. Guide dogs.   2. Human-animal relationships.   I. Fidelco Guide Dog
Foundation.   II. Title.
HV1780.H57 2010
362.4'183—dc22   2009041429

Printed in the United States of America
Designed by Nancy Resnick

For Charlie and Robbie Kaman.
Without your fifty years of vision, hard work, support, and love
there would be no Fidelco.
Thank you from the Fidelco family.

ACKNOWLEDGMENTS

When we began work on this book, we were amateurs. We still are. A world of thanks to the following people.

To David Shanks, CEO of Penguin Books and Clare Ferraro, President of Viking/Plume, for giving us the extraordinary opportunity to tell the Fidelco story in such a meaningful way. To Alessandra Lusardi, our editor, who so graciously "showed us the ropes" and kept us on track. To Gerri Hirshey, who immersed herself in the world of guide dogs and people with visual disabilities and weaved together a masterful story of hope, freedom, and opportunity. To the Fidelco clients who gave us their time, candor, and passion and to the Fidelco staff who shared with us their stories and expertise. To Jack Hayward, who kept the bits and pieces moving. And finally, to the Fidelco family: our clients, volunteers, and supporters who are the fabric of our organization. Thank you for believing in us. We love you and hope you enjoy this wonderful book. We encourage you to continue sharing the vision.

Christine Buhler, director of development
Fidelco Guide Dog Foundation, Inc.
March 2010

AUTHOR ACKNOWLEDGMENTS

Given the siege stage of journalism these days, it has been a pleasure and a privilege to work on a resolutely "good news" story such as Fidelco's, and I thank Jack Hayward and Christine Buhler for giving me that opportunity. As always, a hat tip to my agent Flip Brophy, who knows a good match when she sees one. Thank you, Alessandra Lusardi, for the sensible and sensitive edit.

The entire staff at Fidelco was generous, helpful, and patient during my forays through the kennels and beyond. John Byfield, who pioneered and honed the unique training system, kindly invited me into his Florida home to spool out the origins of the Fidelco Way. Special thanks to the crew in Bloomfield who withstood my repeated sallies: Dave Darr, Jason Stankoski, Becky Cook, Tara Meier-Wilson, Sue Holt Brown, and, for the "fieldwork," Tommy Mourad. The Fidelco guide dog recipients and foster families who shared their stories were a writer's dream: honest, open, and generous with their time. Deepest appreciation to Todd Higgins; Mary Mancuso; Gail Gunn; Nina Bektic and Jose Marrero; Charlene Picard; Marie Russo and her children, Courtney and Eddie Tabor; Vicky and Eamonn Nolan;

Janet and Russell LaBreck; and David Bearden with his amazing, ever-growing family of daughters, grandkids, and adopted and foster sons. And oh, the dogs I met. They are magnificent.

Robbie and Charlie Kaman are the beating heart of American philanthropy: constant, inventive, open-handed, and deeply, quietly committed. Whether sizing up a puppy or counseling clients, Robbie operates in an enviable state of grace—albeit muddy and paw-printed. Spending time with her is a joy.

Finally, thanks to my family—Mark, Sam, and Lila—for their sweet forbearance while Mom went to the dogs.

CONTENTS

TRUST
THE
DOG

PROLOGUE:
TRUST THE DOG

On June 20, 1983, a litter of five male German shepherd puppies was whelped at the kennels of the Fidelco Guide Dog Foundation in Bloomfield, Connecticut. Two days later, the greedily nursing pups had yet to open their eyes when darkness descended on a happy, outgoing nineteen-year-old college student from Killingworth, a small town in a rural part of the state.

As a freshman, Todd Higgins had been deeply engaged with his studies in aviation mechanics at a Florida university and was looking forward to a career in aeronautics. He was back north enjoying his summer break when he was in a serious car accident and caught his final, terrifying glimpse of the visual world. Todd doesn't like to revisit that moment. But he is effusive—bordering on evangelical—when he talks about the puppy from that litter that would help him redirect his shattered life. The dog's name was Promise. He was about eighty pounds, coal black, playfully affectionate, and very serious about his job. And Todd has no doubt their destinies were preordained.

"Promise was born for me," he says.

But both had long and challenging journeys ahead of them before they came together as a team. After eighteen months in the home of a volunteer foster family who exposed him to as much of the busy, noisy human world as possible, Promise would head back to Fidelco for a rigorous six months' training to become a guide dog. The teenager's path was far steeper, fraught with physical and emotional trauma.

After a three-and-a-half-week coma induced by severe head injuries, Todd awoke in the head trauma unit of Hartford Hospital. His eyes were bandaged, but he had miraculously escaped brain damage. It was too soon, doctors told him, to predict the fate of his vision. By August, the contusions had faded and a badly injured leg had begun to heal. But when the surgeon who had tried to repair the impact injuries to both retinas reexamined Todd, he concluded that the damage was too severe to attempt sight-restoring surgery. Two months after the accident, Todd was declared permanently blind.

"It was devastating," he recalls. "The emotion that came up was a lot of anger—really just feeling very helpless and angry. I was a person who, just a couple of months before, was able to go where I wanted, do what I wanted, had every opportunity available to me. And suddenly I was someone who had really limited opportunity or, I felt, no opportunity at all. And I didn't have any clue of what my next step would be."

In late summer, he notified his college that he would be withdrawing. And he found that just getting from room to room in the house he had grown up in suddenly seemed as impossible as that career in aeronautics. As the youngest of five children, he had plenty of help when he settled back into his mother's home in Killingworth. "My family was great. My mother and brothers and sisters were extremely supportive of anything I needed and helped me out in many ways, meeting my physical needs, getting things for me, setting up the services for the blind. The frustration came with the fact that I couldn't do any of it myself—right down to going to the kitchen and making a sandwich. Or getting across the room and out the front door by myself. Everything is oddly familiar but it's not the same because you can't function. I forged ahead and tried to find things, my bedroom, the kitchen."

But he always stopped at the front door. Going "out there" was a terrifying prospect. He would come to think and speak of it as walking off a cliff. He found that the anxiety of sudden blindness was a relentless and powerful jailer. "I couldn't go anywhere independently. At nineteen, you've got that independence for the first time and then you get it pulled away. I certainly lashed out at family members and people around me. I think they understood and it was okay. But it was a hard time for everybody."

His mother and siblings had to return to their jobs and families, but Todd could not be left alone all day. At seventy-eight, having retired to Florida, Todd's maternal grandmother, Doria Gustafson—Nan to her grandchildren—heard the distress call and reported for duty. "She was the matriarch of the family, very independent-thinking, very strong, with an attitude of 'Just pull yourself up by the bootstraps and get on with it,'" Todd says. "She was always the one in our family who would go wherever she was needed. She was an amazing person. She never had any formal education in rehab or anything, but she just knew what to do. She insisted, 'We're going to do these things and this is how you're going to get going again.'" She and Todd's mother, Theodora—Teddy—formed a formidable team. "Nan was the more tough-love part of the team, with my mother's encouragement taking a softer, gentler approach," Todd says. "The result was that I was pushed to keep moving forward, while at the same time having the feeling of strong protection if I felt things were falling apart around me."

It did not take Nan long to impose an unorthodox but strict new regime with a simple philosophy: whatever works.

"First, she had me learn all the capitals of the states and countries of the world. It had me thinking, 'Okay, how can I master this?' That was the beginning of 'Hey, there's something I can do. I still have a mind. I can't see, but there are other parts of me that work pretty well—still.' She just did things to keep my mind occupied and keep me focused on things other than myself and this situation. She helped me engage in activities that showed there were things that I could do and have success."

He admits that, initially, he didn't always grasp the method behind her apparent madness.

"Nan, are you kidding me? Typing? I'm blind."

"You just can't sit there in this chair. Come over here. You're going to learn how to type. You're going to need to know how to do this when you go back to college."

She has bought a manual on touch typing. And she stands over Todd, gently placing his fingers on the correct home keys. A-S-D-F . . . They are at it day after day until he finally masters a basic sentence:

The lazy dog jumped over the red fox.

Call it Todd's Helen Keller moment—perhaps not as earthshaking as the first time Keller spelled "water" in sign language for her teacher. But the small accomplishment tele-

graphs a future. More is possible—a lot more. The clacking gets more rapid and rhythmic as the two of them fall into an intimate, if occasionally turbulent, daily routine.

Breakfast, made by Nan, is followed by morning mind calisthenics.

"Norway?"

"Oslo."

"Venezuela?"

"Caracas."

"Too easy. Sri Lanka."

Weekdays, she leads him to the car and drives him to physical therapy to strengthen his injured leg. Every day after therapy, they joke, "Wherever shall we go for lunch?" And every day, they hit Burger King and return home for another, more pleasant form of rehab: extreme, endless cribbage. Todd has been learning Braille, and with a deck of Braille playing cards, he is soon nimbly moving cribbage pegs, finding the jack of diamonds by touch, matching wits with the flinty old woman who minces no words whenever he sinks into choppy waters.

"Stop feeling sorry for yourself. Get up and get going."

"The future isn't going to come to you."

"Try again. Failure's not fatal."

Todd won't listen to TV now that he can't watch—until Nan hooks him on the arcana of Jeopardy! *and the word-play in* Wheel of Fortune. *Now the boy is being stubborn about listening to books on tape to fill the hours after dinner. He sees it as more capitulation—another sorry indication that he can't read printed books anymore. She sits him down and slides in a Stephen King tape, and at last, he listens. Night after night, they get deliciously creeped out together. And he's hooked. They move on to* Jaws. *Reading is crucial, she keeps telling him.*

"You'll need it when you go back to college."

"Education was very important to her," Todd says. "It wasn't like she was asking me, 'Are you going back to college?' It was always 'When you go back.'" Doria Gustafson would stay with her grandson for the first three years of his recovery, and moved back north permanently. "She lived to be a hundred and one," Todd says. "She was a huge driving force in that tough time. It was never a question, but assumed as fact: You're going to go on with your life and be productive. That's just what's going to happen. Sometimes I would fight her, but she wasn't easy to push around. She was a good strong person for me and that's exactly what I needed to go forward instead of falling backward."

Their routine was interrupted for a course of rehabilitation at the Carroll Center for the Blind in Newton, Massachusetts, where Todd was enrolled as soon as his health permitted. The prospect terrified him. "Deep down inside, I didn't have the confidence to take the next step. There was so much fear and anger. There's a physical fear of the next step—falling off a cliff, falling down the stairs. All those things keep you imprisoned in your own mind."

With a good many misgivings, he went to the Carroll Center. And straightaway, his worst fears were realized. "The first day I got there, I got my new cane. I had no idea how to use it properly. I hadn't had cane mobility instruction before. I was in my room, which happened to be near the top of the staircase. The bathroom was across the hallway. I was trying to use this cane to get across the hall to the bathroom and missed and went tumbling down the stairs."

He was injured, having badly wrenched his leg. Thus his first day at rehab began with an ambulance trip to Newton Hospital. "The whole experience was totally freaky. There I was in a completely unfamiliar area, in an ambulance and then a hospital with only strangers around me. It was really nerve-racking. My sister and brother drove up to be with me a couple of hours later. I had to wear a knee brace for a bit. So that was the first experience trying to venture out from home and be independent." Todd can allow himself a short, dry laugh about it now. "Yeah, I fell off the cliff."

When he returned from the hospital, he was in pain and very, very angry. "The one person I focused the anger on was my mobility instructor. I was pretty short with her. Because of my lack of skill and confidence to go out and travel, I think I kind of shut down during that training. I felt they were pushing me too hard to do something I wasn't comfortable with and didn't have the skill to do. They would do things like take you into a neighborhood and just drop you and say, 'Okay, find your way to a point you're familiar with.' It was terrifying. After falling down the stairs, it was even harder. But that's what you do to learn. You start to use your hearing—okay, I hear this busy street over here, this must be such-and-such street. You learn to orient yourself."

But he was in a very alien setting. The roar of this new world around him was strange and intimidating. "I grew up in Killingworth, which is very rural. And here I am just outside of Boston, inundated with a lot of stimuli and noise and traffic. That's one of the things that is most difficult initially about losing your sight. All this sensory data that you're taking in is suddenly overwhelming."

His counselor at Carroll heard the fury and the frustration in their sessions. "They modified my mobility training and did more country walking with me. Eventually I got the skills I needed to get. They saw where I was and dialed it back a little bit. Then we moved forward."

Interaction with others in the program—the newly blind—reassured Todd that his feelings were not uncommon. The majority of his fellow students had lost their vision to complications from diabetes. One young man had suffered a brain tumor. Another was a victim of the violence in Lebanon, where he had lost his sight in a bomb blast. Todd realized, "I'm not the only one who's going through that anger cycle."

Even as his emotions leveled, cane travel continued to be his bête noire. He credits the depth of the program for turning things around. "The curriculum is much more than the cane. You're cooking, doing kitchen chores, learning to read Braille—and yes, typing. There's a woodworking shop. So you start to build confidence that you can do other things. There was sensory training class, where you really learn how to use your other senses to tune in and process external stimuli more effectively. All those things helped me to be more confident and feel more secure in trying to do cane travel. So I did get to a point where I could travel with a cane and feel like I had a certain level of security. But I wouldn't say I left the Carroll Center thinking I was going to tackle the world with a white cane."

Nor was he disposed to try. Once he returned to his mother's home in Killingworth, he would not go anywhere alone. For half a year, he only ventured out with the supportive eyes—and elbows—of family or the high school friends who visited regularly and began taking him out to meals and movies. He hated the dependency, but was unable to overcome it until he got some advice from another visually impaired person who was able to tap into the fear and frustration that was holding Todd back. "Marvin Burr, my vocational rehabilitation counselor at the Board of Education Services for the Blind, had a Fidelco guide dog. He suggested I apply for one." Marvin Burr was on the board of Fidelco, the only guide dog organization in New England and the first nationwide to pioneer In-Community Placement, which trains visually impaired people with German shepherd dogs where they live and work, rather than in a residential-school setting. Apart from a small application fee, the dogs and the training are donated free of charge.

When Todd applied for a dog in early summer 1984, he interviewed with John Byfield, who had trained guide dogs for over fifteen years before he designed and implemented the innovative training program at Fidelco. John was frank with Todd, as he was with all applicants: Guide dogs aren't for everyone. Caring for them is a huge commitment. And learning to work with a dog would be hard work at first, exhausting and often frustrating. How did he think the dog might change his life? Did he have goals for himself—maybe going back to school or work?

Then John and Todd did what is known in the guide dog community as the "Juno walk." Holding a harness, effectively taking the place of a dog, John had Todd grasp the handle and walk along so that he could assess his gait and speed—the better to match him with just the right dog. Promise was ready for Todd in early December of that year. He would be training with John and Dave Darr, Fidelco's first apprentice trainer; Todd moved in with his sister and brother-in-law in East Hartford for the three weeks of intense training, reasoning that an urban setting would afford better practice with sidewalks, curbs, and traffic than his mother's rural home.

The first day of training was spent getting acquainted with Promise—and with Todd's goals for their partnership. His instructors had lots of questions. What places did he want to go to with the dog? Was there a wish list of things he'd like to do independently again? And most important: Did he feel ready to let the dog take over the navigation duties? The Fidelco team made it very clear that the first step in this new partnership is the hardest and the most essential:

"You have to trust the dog."

Get to that place, they told Todd, and the dog will never let you down. Give it over to him, and he will keep you from all the cliffs: traffic, stairs, obstacles—even fear itself.

Day one went well, and Todd's family members received some firm instructions: No petting, feeding, or caring for the dog by anyone other than Todd during the critical bonding period. No exceptions. The instructors left Promise to settle into his first night of an eight-year working partnership—and a lifelong bond. Unlike some young dogs newly parted from their trainers, he did not howl, pace, or whine. Promise threw up. "I guess he was a little anxious," says Todd. "But so was I."

Day two, and the new team is ready for its first try at independent travel. Main Street in East Hartford bristles with hustle and honk as Promise and Todd step out for their inaugural downtown walk. Dave Darr is walking a watchful five paces behind as they are about to cross the street.

Promise has halted properly at the curb for Todd to get his bearings, locate the curb edge with his right foot, and prepare to step down; the dog has looked in all directions and is about to go forward when suddenly he stops short. Todd hears a sickeningly familiar sound—the squeal of tires and a long skid.

The car that sped out from between two buildings had been undetected by both men, but the dog alerted to it in time. Dave confirms what Todd suspects; it would have likely been a direct hit. But there's an upside to the experience: this dog is young, but now they know he's rock solid.

Once his legs stop shaking, Todd is ready to continue training. And he is thinking: "This is exactly what I need. I'm going to be safe with this dog."

Promise lived up to his name. Todd says that trusting his new partner became implicit as their deep bond developed. And it allowed him to start thinking about a productive future again. He enrolled in some classes at nearby Middlesex Community College in January 1985, as soon as he had finished training with Promise. "Having that training experience and being confident of traveling alone gave me a lot of encouragement to get back into school. I took classes at Middlesex for a year and a half while living at home. Then I was accepted at the University of Connecticut. Promise was a big part of my being emotionally ready to say, 'I think I can do this'—leave home alone, live in a dorm, get around a big campus. Having the dog helped me be able to say, 'Okay, I'm going to move on from here.'"

The crippling sense of isolation began to fall away as the two of them negotiated a wider world and became a solid team. Todd says that the essential bond the Fidelco instructors had talked about was his greatest balm. "The dogs are so in tune with you, in every way. Particularly when you're physically ill, have the flu or something. You'll be lying on the couch, feeling like death warmed over, and the dog is suddenly beside you, giving you comfort. Even if you're just emotionally upset, they come to you and give you comfort because they know you're hurting. That's happened with all the dogs I've had."

Likewise, he became deeply sensitized to the animal's emotional and physical condition. "You can feel a dog's tension or stress through a harness. When you get to a stressful situation, very crowded, with a lot of noise, you feel a tautness in the harness, you can feel them going into this ultra-dialed-in mode. If you're in an airport or a train terminal, their whole affect is changed. Every muscle in their body is on heightened alert. They're taking everything in, their heads swivel, their ears go straight back."

As college roomies, Todd and Promise navigated serpentine paths throughout the vast campus, made friends, and hosted a parade of readers willing to help, since Todd's new Braille skills were not up to the speed required for advanced courses. After graduation from UConn, Todd's experiences getting the services and accommodations he needed to be a successful college student led to a career in disability advocacy. "I found a job working at the Connecticut Office of Protection and Advocacy for Persons with Disabilities—mainly with vocational rehabilitation for people who wanted to enter the workforce."

Several years into his career and his partnership with Promise, Fidelco provided Todd with another life partner. Maureen O'Connor was managing the Fidelco bike-a-thon fundraiser when they met. The announcement for their marriage in 1993 informed guests that the celebration would also be a retirement party for Promise, who attended the seaside ceremony in a white bow tie and stepped out of harness a month later at age ten and a half—a good, long run for a guide dog. It was an excruciating decision for Todd, but as ever, Promise helped him get there. He had long been able to tap into the deep, if unspoken, wisdom of the dog.

"You get these close times when you're brushing or grooming

them," Todd explains. "It's a silent but perfect communication. Something happened where Promise let me know that he was ready to not work anymore. The way he would hang his head—he was tired, you could tell. I sometimes see people in the guide dog world work their dogs to really old age. I think it's a fine line between being cruel and understanding. You have to put your own selfish needs aside. Of course you don't want to lose this companion that's so close to you, that has given you all this loyalty. But you have to recognize that you need to let go and release the dog from its duty. It's a tough thing to do, but it's important for people to keep in touch with how the dog is doing. It's just a gut feeling when you know, because of that bond you have."

Promise lived his final few years with Todd, Maureen, their pet dog, and Todd's second Fidelco dog, Urrick. "They got along great," Todd says. "Promise would lick Urrick's ears—he was almost like a mentor to him."

A shepherd named Gustav followed Urrick, and Todd is now partnered with his fourth Fidelco dog, Zeb. Half of the hundred dogs the foundation now places each year are "successor" dogs to those retired from Fidelco or other guide dog schools. In 2004, Todd accepted a position with the State of California's Protection Advocacy Agency under a new grant program designed to help people who have suffered traumatic brain injury and other head traumas to access needed services. Based in Sacramento, Todd and Zeb travel the state, sometimes to the mammoth Balboa Naval Hospital in San Diego to work with severely injured soldiers.

It is a purposeful, active life. "Fidelco has given me a wife and four dogs—and with them, my work," Todd says. "All these gifts are priceless. And I don't ever try to imagine the life I might have had without them."

Since 1981, over 1,200 visually impaired people in thirty-five states and Canada have reclaimed their independence, partnered with Fidelco German shepherds. The foundation's name is a combination of two words predicated on trust: "fidelity," faithfulness to commitments, and "cooperative," done in cooperation with others.

The Fidelco mission had its origin two decades earlier, in 1960, as the nonprofit Fidelity Breeders Cooperative. Charlie Kaman, a world-renowned aeronautics inventor and executive, and his wife, Robbie (short for Roberta and pronounced RO-bee), a respected dog breeder and handler, began raising German shepherd dogs in central Connecticut and donating them to guide dog schools and police departments. The Kamans renamed their program the Fidelco Guide Dog Foundation in 1981, when they decided to include training and placement of the dogs they raised.

From the beginning, they knew they could not launch their charitable endeavor without help—a lot of help. And today, hundreds of unpaid volunteers stand behind each donated dog: fund-raisers, donors, and foster individuals and families who raise the puppies in their homes from the time the dogs are eight weeks old until they are about fourteen to sixteen months, when they are ready for training. Others adopt retired guide and breed dogs. The foundation is financed solely from private contributions and fund-raisers; Fidelco receives no United Way, state, federal, or local government funding.

One of Fidelco's most steadfast supporters is the Lions Club, still faithful to a direct challenge issued by Helen Keller when she addressed the group's national convention in 1925. Seeking support for the newly formed American Foundation for the

Blind, Keller wound up her address by asking the Lions: "Will you not constitute yourselves Knights of the Blind in this crusade against darkness?" In programs reaching 205 countries, Lions Clubs now fund eye banks, vision screenings, eyeglass recycling, and programs to combat vision-destroying diseases such as African river blindness.

At Fidelco's annual spring open house, Lions members representing chapters from all over New England line up, checks in hand, to present funds raised at car washes, bake sales, golf tournaments, and charity walks. There are large gifts, such as vans for transporting the dogs. And there are smaller, more sustained acts of kindness: in one Vermont town, the Lions chapter quietly covers the food and veterinary costs of a needy woman's Fidelco guide dog.

How much can it cost to get a life back? It currently requires an average of $26,000 to breed, raise, train, and place each guide dog, and keep it in top form with regular evaluations and skill tune-ups. And unlike most guide dog schools, which require a month-long residential training period at their facilities, Fidelco's in-community method sends instructor-trainers to all clients' homes and workplaces to integrate the dog into their lives, work, and communities. As conceived by the Kamans and John Byfield, the Fidelco system rests on an ongoing commitment to clients, who are reassured with this open invitation: "Call us anytime." Relocating from the country to the city? A trainer will be there long ahead of the moving van to smooth the transition—as he or she will be for the life of the dog. And the next one.

Fidelco's dogs are all German shepherds, from a "breed within a breed" line specially developed by Robbie Kaman and her animal husbandry staff. Over the last fifty years, American dogs have been selectively bred with strong, hard-working Bavarian stock imported from Germany. There are Fidelco shepherds to suit a wide range of personalities and needs. Small, agile females can fold themselves beneath an airplane seat—in coach. Fast-paced, powerful males can relish city subway work and won't quail at a holiday crowd in Times Square or the darting squirrels and humans of busy Boston Common. Their coats can be coal black or black-and-tan, long-haired or normal coated. Some gentle, easygoing shepherds are well suited to elementary school classrooms, families with young children, or slower-paced elderly clients. Fidelco shepherds accompany their users to high schools and colleges, law schools, boardrooms, recording studios, and high-level government meetings.

Most of their human partners will tell you they are astounded at the suitability of their canine matches, how quickly and deeply the bond forms, and how they grow together. They report moments that defy conventional logic:

How is it that an untrained puppy, fostered by a family with a seriously disabled child, can alert the parents to an impending seizure—before sensitive medical instruments sound the alarm?

How did a retired guide dog working in a rural area grow into his second career as a therapy dog for abused children in an inner city?

What sensory input allows a guide dog to predict his handler's insulin imbalance and place his body in front of her so that she cannot move—seconds before her diabetic collapse?

The stories in this book are true but astonishing, tragic and triumphant, highly improbable—yet perfectly believable as they unfold. In the words of one Fidelco client, "I'm in a perpetual state of amazement. You just can't make this stuff up." And the testimonies that follow speak to these wonders. In the eight to ten years of active guide work, these dogs save lives and dignity, restore independence, and jump-start ambitions. They can steady family dynamics knocked sideways by visual impairment. And they retire with the comforts and respect accorded to heroes.

No guide dog partnerships are perfect, or exactly alike. Yet all depend on an earned and deepening trust. That interspecies fidelity began at the dawn of the dog's domestication. Guide dogs have been used since the 1920s in Germany, when war injuries left a large corps of soldiers with visual impairments. And they are still the mainstay of a burgeoning new age of service animals—from capuchin monkeys assisting quadriplegics to miniature horses that act as guides and companions. Dogs that proved unsuited to guide work are now being "repurposed" to help children cope with autism, with miraculous effect. As science is probing exciting and provocative new areas for service animals, outdated disability laws are being debated and rewritten. And human rights activism is pushing toward fuller accessibility for all.

As Fidelco marks its fiftieth anniversary, no one attending births in the lively "puppy house," dispensing chow in the kennels, or tramping eight to ten miles a day training dogs in communities has much time or inclination for self-congratulation. Fidelco understands that the imperative is growing. According to a recent study by Prevent Blindness America, 30 million Americans are afflicted with potentially blinding eye disorders. And as baby boomers age, the population will experience a significant rise in vision-impacting conditions such as diabetes and macular degeneration. More guide dogs will be needed. And there are still plenty of obstacles to clear.

Those who live, work with, and love visually impaired men and women understand that Fidelco's unique history can hardly play as a soft-focus critter flick, all bouncing pups and beatitude.

Uplifting as they may be, the stories in this book begin in the dark and its implacable isolation. Guide dogs and their users must function in a world that is not always hospitable and often harrowing.

Sighted readers of this book may find the journeys of these human/canine partners uplifting, revelatory, shocking, disturbing—even shaming. We just have no idea what it's like. Any sighted person who spends hours listening to and walking with persons who are blind must scale a pretty steep learning curve. As the full picture emerges, it's clear we must come to terms with our own stubborn myopias—personal, cultural, governmental—that still cause the unsighted to stumble.

Discrimination, misinformation, and simple misunderstanding still challenge the best of guide dog teams. The most prevalent and persistent threat—attacks by unleashed dogs—is a thoughtless human failing. So it's hardly surprising that some of the most successful guide dog users have become tireless advocates for the rights of the disabled.

When he was first training with Promise, Todd Higgins sometimes had the company of another newly blind teenager. Mary Mancuso (then Mary Hook) was just eighteen when diabetic retinopathy, complicated by glaucoma and unsuccessful surgery, left her completely blind. Soon after, she was paired with a fluffy, long-haired male Fidelco shepherd named Nemo. John Byfield and Dave Darr would sometimes take the two teams out together.

The long, tiring days were often leavened with a sly, slightly noirish humor from the instructors and their young charges.

Dutifully, Todd, Mary, and the dogs plunged on in teeming rainstorms at John's directive—only to find out much later that he was always directing things from beneath an umbrella. Eager to learn how to traverse the huge roadside piles of snow characteristic of New England winters, Mary insisted on tackling them, no matter the weather conditions. Nemo slid and tugged and Mary slipped, climbed, and giggled as Dave groused aloud. His student had to get over the obstacles herself. But passing motorists shot him filthy stares—along with a few reprimands flung out of car windows:

"Hey, buddy, how about helping the poor blind lady?"

Mary swears that Nemo had a wicked sense of humor. Early on, he taught her a wry, though ultimately life-saving, lesson about who was trail boss on their wagon train.

Mary and Nemo are a fairly new team, but they are working well, navigating Silas Deane Highway, a busy four-lane thoroughfare through Wethersfield, Connecticut. The big dog is keeping her firmly, safely to the center of the sidewalk as cars whiz noisily by. And then he stops, abruptly.

"Forward," Mary commands.

Nemo stays put.

"Nemo, forward!"

Maybe there is an obstacle—maybe she should tell him "find the way" so he'll take her around whatever it is. But no, she's going with her own judgment here, and this time, her voice is loud and insistent.

"Forward!"

Nemo gives in and proceeds straight ahead. Suddenly,

Mary is drenched. A sprinkler. She couldn't hear its hiss beneath the traffic. She stands there, dripping and shaking with laughter. It's benign, it's funny. But this is the last time she'll fail to trust the dog.

Thus she is not inclined to doubt Nemo a few years later when, after a heavy overnight thunderstorm, they head out for an early morning walk in Windsor, not far from Fidelco headquarters, where she has begun to work as a liaison to other vision-impaired "graduates" like her. They are on a quiet street, walking at a relaxed pace, when Nemo stops short again and cuts in front of her, pulling her off course and to the side. He is so firm—Mary can sense his tension—that she decides to turn around and go back. Since she likes to check on such unusual behavior, she asks a friend—a mobility instructor—to return to the spot with her and see what stopped the dog. Nearing the place, her friend gasps.

"I don't believe it."

Just past the spot Nemo had stopped, a live electrical wire downed by the storm dangles at chest level.

Nemo was named Guide Dog of the Year in 1989 by the Delta Society, an animal advocacy group, and the American Animal Hospital Association, comprising 10,000 veterinarians. The live-wire incident was just one of the things cited in his nomination. In many ways, Nemo was a loving and vigilant protector for a young woman with more than her share of health problems. When Mary's diabetes caused an insulin imbalance and she fainted at a bus stop, Nemo lay down next to her, head and paws on her body, and would not move. The sight of a large, long-haired German shepherd guarding her did cause some consternation among the EMT workers, until animal control officers took him gently into custody and Mary could be loaded into the ambulance.

"Nemo was always good medicine," she says. When Mary underwent a kidney transplant in 1987 and became alarmingly despondent in the hospital, her then-husband Ken Hook got permission to bring Nemo to her bedside. Without ever having been there, the dog all but dragged Ken down the corridors and straight to her room, where he leaped onto the bed. And when he was given permission to stay with Mary, her condition improved dramatically. Debera Palmeri, one of her transplant nurses, provided testimony for the award nomination: "In a real sense, Nemo has given Mary back the kind of active life a young woman should have."

And how Mary loved him. She says she couldn't have imagined the dimensions of his gifts. "I really didn't understand how a dog would change your life and give you that sense of freedom and independence. As much as I had people tell me, until I experienced it, I couldn't grasp it. It just gave me a purpose. I had a dog helping me—and I had to help him. He gave me so much and I gave him his basic needs. But always with full love and devotion and caring."

She thinks he was fine with the transaction: "When a dog is bred to work and they love it, it just shows. Nemo loved to work. He was happy to see his harness come out."

Eventually, her fragile health forced Mary to give up her work as a public speaker and ambassador (with Nemo) for Fidelco, appearing with John Byfield at schools, civic groups, and fund-raisers, as well as her work in the office. Nemo retired after ten years in harness, and there have been three more dogs. Her current companion, Lobo, came to her after the sudden death of a friend of Mary's who had been partnered with him.

"They've all been good dogs, but there was no dog like Nemo," she says of the one who gave her back her life. "A lot of people feel that way about the first dog, when life changes so much for the better. The first is the miracle dog. But with the other three—it was never as hard to trust them as it was the first. Nemo saw to that."

The end of a partnership, she admits, is never easy. Todd Higgins agrees. He says he has learned to give himself time to grieve and adjust before beginning training with the next dog. It's only fair. He still chokes up when he describes the stubborn service of his second dog, Urrick, who had been diagnosed with inoperable cancer and was on a medication to shrink the tumor when Todd tried to do the humane thing and retire him.

It was clear the dog still wanted to work; keeping him out of harness was making him stressed and unhappy. Since Urrick's cancer medication did not affect cognitive function, the specialists at Angell Animal Medical Center in Boston told Todd, "By all means, let him keep working, if that's what he wants."

The family dogs—Urrick and the Higginses' massive 160-pound Newfoundland, Charlie—just love car rides, so all four of them go on what they expect to be a quick trip to Danbury, Connecticut, where Maureen, a real estate agent, has a property closing. Suddenly, billowing smoke is enveloping them in the parking lot where they've left their car. An adjacent building is ablaze and the lot has filled with fire equipment and smoke. They are trapped, and so is their car.

Police and fire personnel begin to lead them out when Urrick simply takes charge. Maureen is leading Charlie out on his leash as Urrick steps calmly forward, tail down, ears back, peering carefully beneath the lowering smoke clouds at the ground.

He is pulling Todd forward painstakingly through the tangle of thick, pulsing hoses, pausing for the man to feel each one with a foot, step over and pause for the next. The dog is purposeful and steady beneath the clamor, smoke, and chaos, and when they are safely out, it is apparent that Urrick is the only one needing medical attention. Clearly, the effort has caused him pain and fatigue. An emergency trip to a Danbury veterinarian confirms the Higginses' fears. Despite his flawless performance, the dog's condition has gotten appreciably worse. What's left of his life will likely be filled with great pain and suffering.

Back home the following morning, Urrick dies peacefully with the ministrations of the family veterinarian.

Todd stops for a moment to compose himself as he describes the dog's dedication. "He was guiding, he was totally on board, as if to say, *Hey, this is my job, I've got it covered.* So he guided me out of this horrendous situation and he did a perfect job—right up to the end."

As longtime partners with Fidelco guide dogs, Todd and Mary have watched the foundation grow with pride and affection. "It's family," Mary says. "And they've taken so many of us such a long, long way forward."

This is a book about a half century's worth of such trials, journeys, and transformations, about the miracles and mysteries of these deep partnerships—and about the dedication, skill, and training that make them possible. And although many charitable organizations are currently struggling to maintain support and services, the difficult economic climate is also an encouraging stress test for the state of American volunteerism. As Robbie Kaman puts it, "You won't believe some of the things that people do for us." You won't forget them, either.

CHAPTER ONE

DOG PEOPLE

I've never been without a dog.

—Robbie Kaman

It is an auspicious Sunday morning in 1963 as Charlie Kaman pilots his mammoth blue four-door Lincoln out of the cargo area at New York International Airport with its long-awaited bit of baggage peering out the back window. She is a young shepherd named Alma Kirschental, a breeding female he has purchased from Karl Fuller, a sheep herder and dog breeder who raised her on his farm in Bavaria.

In the back of the car, Alma is calm and relaxed after her long journey in the plane's roaring belly. Charlie knows that Alma is a prize; Karl Fuller had been reluctant to part with such an exemplar of the strong, loyal, and talented herding stock he relies on. But the ever-expanding Haus of Fuller has been clamoring for indoor plumbing.

And so the deal was cut: for the price of a Bavarian loo, about four hundred dollars (which included shipping), Alma would be flown to Charlie Kaman and the Fidelity Breeders Cooperative, his fledgling German shepherd program in Connecticut.

It's nearly lunchtime as they head back home. Charlie's young son Bill is in the front seat, and he is hungry. When his father pulls into a busy restaurant parking lot, Bill is out the door before Charlie can grab him, darting between parked and moving cars.

And here is Alma, bolting out the open door and after the child. She overtakes him easily and places her sturdy frame in his path. Charlie catches up with them both, relieved and amazed as he hugs his boy.

Did the dog think Bill was a sheep? Was she just that intelligent, that natural and formidable a herder? Whatever the genetic witchcraft at work here, Charlie is now convinced: with Alma and her progeny, he can raise some exceptional shepherds—working dogs, like this Bavarian wonder, with a hardwired instinct to protect and serve.

"The incident with Alma was mind-blowing," says Robbie Kaman. "This dog had just come off an airplane. She didn't know the child or anybody else." She recalls Charlie's excitement at finding himself possessed of a sturdy, breedable link toward the ultimate working dog—the sort they might raise and donate to guide dog schools and police departments. He tells her: "This is a once-in-a-lifetime kind of dog."

Robbie is a compact, soft-spoken woman in her early seventies blessed with considerable wealth—and completely uninterested in its material trappings. She will tell you that her greatest fortune is in her work, and she mines it with gusto. She is here now at Fidelco as she is every single day, unpaid, in neat, no-nonsense kennel attire. And she is everywhere: in the puppy house, the kennels, hacking up meat in the kitchen, consulting with veterinarians, fielding phone questions from fosters or guide dog users and—when she absolutely must as president and chairman of the board—presiding in the Fidelco conference room.

So respected is Robbie's breeding and training expertise that she was persuaded to give a genetics presentation at the International Federation of Guide Dog Schools conference in England in 1992. But she was happy to get it over with and get back to the kennels. This is a woman known to walk through the office carrying a surgical tray with a large diseased dog spleen just removed by a veterinarian. "Isn't this something?" she trilled to rapidly retreating backs. As anyone at Fidelco can attest, Robbie is perfectly at peace just washing a puppy.

She was a lifelong dog fancier and trainer in 1960 when she joined a German shepherd club in New Haven and met Charlie Kaman, her future husband and founder of Kaman Corporation. (Charlie's previous marriage, which produced three children, ended in divorce.) Robbie and Charlie would work together with German shepherds for just over a decade before they married in 1971. She explains how they both came to be devoted to the breed:

"I had been showing poodles and also had a golden retriever. I had done a lot of work with obedience training and I was interested in a dog that liked to work. It was for that reason that I looked to the shepherd. Its history was basically as a working dog and a very people-oriented dog. It liked to work." Robbie got her first shepherd, a female, in 1957 from a New Haven breeder who had brought dogs from Germany. "She was small and long-haired. Cute as cute could be. I raised her and trained her and showed her in obedience classes. She was enough to capture me and get me motivated to work with the breed."

She believes that Charlie's enthusiasm came from his childhood. Born in 1919, Charles H. Kaman grew up in Washington, D.C. His father, Charles W., emigrated from Germany with his family at age two. He became a construction supervisor who helped build Union Station, the Russell Senate Office Building, and the Supreme Court building, among others. And he kept German shepherds when his children were small.

Thus Robbie and Charlie fell into step together as dog people—the sort that fall in thrall with a breed and spend every spare Saturday parsing blood lines and standing in chilly meadows judging fang and flank with similarly besotted humans. Dog people exhibit a high tolerance for sartorial disarray; willingly, they sport a light dusting of dried field mud and dog hair, and the track marks of affectionate slobber. They surrender décor to needle-sharp puppy teeth, and do not blanch at the sight of upchucked chipmunk. For reasons of practicality and temperament, dog people don't wear a lot of black. And if, like Robbie Kaman, their infatuations go beyond hobby to a life's work, they generally wake up happy and carry a certain radiance to the job.

"My work with the shepherd breeding just kind of evolved because I was sort of the get-the-jobs-done type person, hands on, not afraid to get dirty," Robbie says. "I raised the puppies, really managed the livestock. I used to say to Mr. Kaman, 'You need a dedicated, hardworking woman.' That's why he married me." She laughs—as she does often and easily.

Did she know at first that he was a titan of industry, founder of a multimillion-dollar company nestled in the wooded outback of tiny Bloomfield?

"Well, I knew the name."

And when shepherd club confabs were held on the vast acreage of Kaman Corporation, Robbie got a wider angle on this tall, rangy man with an agile, impatient mind and a facility for multitasking decades before the term was coined. Driving through the Kaman gates, she took in the strange circular enclosures called test rigs where helicopter rotor trials could be performed safely; she noted the rows of shiny new choppers outside long gray fabrication buildings. But always, she was focused on the dogs. "People would come over to the plant here and we'd evaluate breeding stock and help people out if they were having problems with their puppies," she remembers. "We always had some kind of a gathering going that involved dogs—almost every weekend."

They observed dogs' physical confirmation and gaits, and watched how they interacted with other dogs and any children present. They compared thoughts on ideal breed characteristics. Science, Robbie had learned early on, was only part of a successful breeder's skill. The rest is ineffable, instinctive. "Sometimes," she says, "it's just an ear for music."

Fidelco's offices and breeding and training facilities were ultimately built where those first German shepherds enjoyed their weekend runs in the Kaman corporate park, on about three acres at the back of a dead-end road. Today's visitors must still drive along a bumpy lane past a massive wooden test rig and rows of new choppers shrink-wrapped in white plastic before pulling up to the long, low building with the cement German shepherd standing guard out front.

Fidelco headquarters are neat and professional—and well stocked with chew toys. Even in the administrative wing, occasional woofs and ruffs erupt from every other office and cubicle—many employees have adopted retired guide and breed dogs, which accompany them to work. There is an oil portrait of Karl Fuller at work in the Bavarian hills in the reception area, which is patrolled by a feisty cat and a venerable retired shepherd who snoozes beneath the desk. Guide dog users calling with questions or problems are often astonished that, as one client put it, "everyone seems to know who you are, and your dog's name. It's like calling family, not some big foundation." But the Kamans—these open-handed dog people— are a most unusual, hands-on pair of public benefactors.

American philanthropy has long been supported by compassionate couples who throw their wealth and energies behind a cause—from John D. and Catherine T. MacArthur's "genius grants" to Bill and Melinda Gates's humanitarian projects. Couples constitute such a vital sector of giving that there are now "Couples Philanthropy Retreats" offering workshops on how to get along with your board—and keep peace with your heirs. Many philanthropic pairs hire expert advisers to help them decide on suitable recipients. The Kamans had no need of such consultancies; the inspiration for their charitable work bounded right up to them with muddy paws and a wet nose.

"What can I tell you?" says Robbie. "Utterly and completely, we've gone to the dogs."

In fact, in 1977, Charlie Kaman cut an LP he titled *Going to the Dogs*. He plays lead and rhythm guitar; a sampling of his considerable skills as an axman can be downloaded from the Internet. On most cuts, he is joined by his sons Bill on rhythm guitar and Steve on drums. There is some barking in the background. Daughter "Beanie" designed the cover, which pictures Charlie holding a shepherd pup. The liner notes include a fund-raising pitch for . . . yes, Fidelco.

Charlie Kaman explained why they decided to raise guide dogs in a 1999 Fidelco annual report: "Robbie and I had a friend whose son was blind. When he received a guide dog, we watched as that amazing animal changed not only the boy's life, but the lives of those around him. Robbie and I had always raised German shepherds because we admired the breed for its natural intelligence, and we donated them for police work because we wanted to give back to society. However, the shepherding dogs we saw in Germany revealed a new possibility for the ultimate in new guide dogs."

Of course, it also took money—lots of money, generated in large part by an industrial empire as idiosyncratic as it has been durable. Though, at ninety, Charlie Kaman's public communications have been silenced by a combination of ailments that plague old age, the very briefest survey of his life's work suggests the kind of unconventional brain most receptive to innovation— be it helicopter rotors or dog training.

A few noteworthy career arcs:

While still a candidate for his degree in aerospace engineering from Catholic University in Washington, D.C., where he would graduate first in his class, Charlie spent one hundred hours building a balsa-wood plane for a contest. In the final round at Constitution Hall, he wound its rubber-band-powered propeller 1,500 times and set an international record for time aloft. He pushed the envelope—wound the next model 3,500 times using an automatic eggbeater—and watched his plane implode. Later he would reflect, "It taught me a lesson in handling disappointment and the need for conservatism and care in all things."

And like any inventor worth his patent fees, he kept going. By the 1990s, a division of his business called Kaman Sciences would provide the technology to track debris in space. The Sciences division also provided information to help U.S. defense personnel guide Scud-seeking Patriot missiles in the Persian Gulf War. In Operation Desert Storm, Kaman Corporation's

Magic Lantern mine detection system helped American troops pick their way through hostile terrain.

As a teenager, Charlie taught himself to play the guitar by ear and gigged around Washington. After winning an audition with Tommy Dorsey's band in an amateur contest run by by Dorsey's sponsor, the Raleigh/Kool cigarette company, the young guitarist got (and turned down) an offer to play in Dorsey's band for a princely seventy-five dollars a week. He said he loved flying machines too much. In the mid-sixties, when the venerable Martin Guitars declined his offer to purchase the company, Charlie developed, patented, and manufactured the Ovation guitar, the now-iconic instrument that melded traditional wood construction with space-age materials in its distinctive rounded back. He just applied some vibration physics learned in crafting helicopter hulls. The roster of musicians who rely on Ovations runs from Glen Campbell to Megadeth, Mötley Crüe, Phil Collins, Melissa Etheridge, Shakira, Ziggy Marley, Aerosmith's Steven Tyler, and Cyndi Lauper.

In 1943, at age twenty-four, Charlie was promoted to head of aerodynamics for the Hamilton Standard division of Connecticut-based United Aircraft, which would become the industry giant United Technologies Corporation. Told there was room for only one inventor there—the helicopter pioneer Igor Sikorsky—Charlie took his ideas to his mother's garage and built a test rig to try out his own dream machines with a 1933 Pontiac engine, the hindquarters of a junked Dodge, and parts from a bathroom scale. It didn't work too well. But by 1951, he had morphed steering and stability innovations from his garage beginnings into the Kaman K-225, the world's first gas-turbine powered copter—now enshrined at the Smithsonian National Air and Space Museum.

It should come as no surprise that Charlie Kaman went about building a better service dog the way he built his machines: he was the tireless dreamer, field marshal, and scout, and Robbie was the gifted, hands-on fabricator. "If he wasn't working on Kaman business seven days a week, he was involved with the dogs at some level," Robbie says. "Training, going to meetings, searching for breeding stock."

Charlie was especially keen on administering the "umbrella test" to young dogs. He carried around a big umbrella he would whip open suddenly before a leashed dog's face. "He used it to gauge a dog's startle response and recovery time," Robbie explains. "Ideally it would have a short recovery and come back to examine this big black thing."

All the while, Charlie had growing challenges to his corporate enterprises. The early sixties were turbulent years for Kaman Aerospace, which had been counting on revenues from a large military procurement contract that Congress and President John F. Kennedy had signed off on in 1963. Five days after JFK's assassination, the Department of Defense, under new president Lyndon Johnson, nixed the deal. Yet the early nuclear age would prove a fertile period for aviation innovators studying the increasingly unfriendly skies. Cold War thunderheads gathered after Nikita Khrushchev famously pounded his shoe at the United Nations, and the Soviets shot down Francis Gary Powers's U-2 spy plane. New and exotic theaters of conflict were requiring more rugged, adaptable flying machines. Kaman Husky choppers had performed more military rescues than any other craft in the Korean War—11,000 personnel saved with no aircraft-caused accidents or loss of life. Soon, more Huskys would be deployed than any other aircraft in the hellish search-and-rescue missions required by the dense jungles and paddies of Vietnam.

And suddenly, shepherd dogs were in demand for a growing homeland service segment. "The early sixties marked the beginning in this country of the use of K9 dogs for police work," Robbie says. "I happened to be involved with the working aspect of the dogs, so naturally I got involved with the people who were developing K9 programs—including the Connecticut State Police. Their first German shepherd dogs came from Fidelco."

The state police had been using bloodhounds, but shepherds proved to be excellent scent and tracking dogs as well. The Kamans' shepherds acquitted themselves so well in the field that by the mid-sixties, Robbie recalls, "some of the surrounding states sent officers to Connecticut to train. And it just mushroomed."

As they produced more puppies than their home facilities could manage, Robbie began a foster program in Connecticut's Litchfield County. High school students raised the puppies at home in a Fidelco/4-H Club partnership. And they, too, realized that they were caring for some remarkable animals. They had plenty of things to tell Mrs. Kaman as she drove up to give their puppies shots, deliver dog food, or hold an obedience class. She never tired of hearing them.

"There were a lot of interesting stories over the years about dogs keeping kids away from the pool or machinery—anything that could be perceived as a threat," she recalls. "The dogs were always very attentive to these things even though they hadn't been taught. They had done it working with the sheep, keeping them out of the road, the pond, a ditch—they just knew these were places where you didn't permit your charges to go. The instinctive nature comes through from that old herding stock, which worked with the master as a team. As many generations as we've come down now, it carries through."

Guide dog schools that received the Kamans' dogs were also reporting excellent results. John Byfield, director of training at Guiding Eyes for the Blind, a residential training school on Long Island, became a regular recipient. And—quickly pegged as another incurable dog person—he was soon a valued member of the Kamans' shaggy circle.

John, a Briton, had first gone to the dogs as a cadet in the London metropolitan police force. He found he enjoyed caring for police dogs, laying scent trails for their training, and hiding himself in urban spider holes to see if they could find him. Drafted into the Royal Navy, he became a K9 handler doing security work in Northern Ireland and Wales for his two-year hitch. He came to the United States in 1964 to become a trainer of guide dogs for the blind at the Long Island school, and within two years he was promoted to director of training there.

Sometimes, when the Kamans needed a demonstration of what their dogs could be trained to do—most often to motivate donors—John Byfield would load one of their fully trained dogs into his car, drive up to Connecticut, and put on a crackerjack show. "He knew how to bring out the best in our shepherds and get them to work to their fullest potential," Robbie says. "It was just thrilling to see them work."

In late 1980, the Kamans had an intriguing conversation with the trainer. He admitted that he had his own ideas on a different kind of guide dog training. And he was looking for a change.

It's 5:30 a.m., and the head of the Kaman Corporation is dressed down—way down—and pulling on his muck boots. In 1981, as his firm is charging hard toward its eight-year run as a Fortune 500 company, all is peaceful on the Kamans' gated, twenty-two-acre spread in Farmington,

Connecticut. But it is rarely quiet, thanks to a flock of fractious sheep kept for Robbie's herding training sideline, a huge Morgan horse, and a constant welter of shepherds—breed dogs, puppies, young adults—bivouacked in the house and grounds.

Charlie works alone for about an hour, as is his habit, shoveling out pens, stables, and kennels, meditative and ankle-deep in the fragrant mire until Robbie grabs a broom to join him. And here, with his own shovel, is the future of the Fidelco Guide Dog Foundation—John Byfield, who has just joined the Kamans to start this new charitable enterprise. He is living in their home until he can find a house nearby and move his family.

The three work together this way for a couple of hours every morning. There are dogs everywhere, in the carport, the barn, the basement—up to forty at once. You can't open a door around this house, Robbie is heard to mutter, without a dog popping out. The place looks like one of those pet-centric George Booth cartoons that run in The New Yorker—hounds nosing at the pantry, puppies upending the flowerpots. And the less said the better about the time Robbie—a tad overworked—forgot a package she had picked up at a local slaughterhouse to use in her special blend of dog food and left it in the trunk of Charlie's car. Perfumed by overripe tripe, the carport was no place for man or beast.

The sun is fully up and it is time for Charlie to scrape his boots, bathe, and climb into the power suit appropriate to an eighties corporate mogul. He looks around at the canine chaos and announces, "We have to do something about this."

Charlie goes to his corporate board with a request and the first Fidelco kennels are built—in a converted copter test rig.

John Byfield recalls his first exposure to Fidelco shepherds at the guide dog school on Long Island. "We had just started a breeding program of Labradors and golden retrievers. But we had no source of German shepherds. To have an offer of dogs who were created from working strains was an absolute bonus. I didn't hesitate. They were sound dogs and they had the desire and the willingness to work. It was a very helpful addition to the program."

He is reminiscing above a bumptious tide of large dogs on his Florida porch: a spirited young standard poodle, a short-haired collie, and a long-haired shepherd, all being trained for guide work. The poodle, he admits, "is a long-term project." At seventy-three, just retired from Fidelco in 2009, John commutes between his family home north of Orlando and western New York State, where he now trains and places animals for Freedom Guide Dogs, a school staffed by some former Fidelco trainers that uses what it calls "hometown placement." Every three weeks or so, he drives a van back and forth—with the three dogs crated and a list of simpatico motel managers along the way.

"Bailey, get your nose off the table. You know better."

John still checks in with and advises Fidelco clients in Florida, as he has done since moving here in the mid-nineties. He figures it's a lifetime responsibility, and he likes to stay in touch. His wife, Pam, is an antique dealer possessed of the exquisite patience required to stay married so long to an extreme dog person. Her voice is serene from within the house:

"John, I believe Captain has had an accident in the kitchen."

Still swabbing after all these years. Throughout a long after-noon of reminiscences, John will be up and down, in and out, with one dog or another—reflexively. He, too, cannot recall being without a dog. Or three.

After a brisk walk around the block with an unabashed Cap-tain, John is recalling the circumstances that drew him to the Kamans' new project. This was in late 1980, when he was still on Long Island, feeling the limits of a residential school. He had some ideas for building a more flexible and effective train-ing program. "One thing that had frustrated me for a long time was that for many people, it just wasn't possible to leave home and work for a month to go and receive a guide dog," he says. "I'd known a number of people who just couldn't get away, and missed out on the independence a dog could offer."

And then, kismet: the call from Charlie Kaman. He and Rob-bie were thinking of expanding beyond breeding to donating fully trained guide dogs. "Charlie asked if I would be interested in joining them. He and Robbie came to Long Island. We had lunch together and went over the particulars—what Charlie's goals were, how I thought I could fit in."

Charlie's dog-scouting odysseys throughout Germany had turned up accounts of an itinerant guide dog trainer who would visit different areas of that country and train people who are blind to use their dogs where they lived. Charlie and Robbie vis-ited the man's school headquarters in Germany and discussed his methods at length. They liked what he had to tell them. It made such perfect sense. And John relayed his own experience: some people who really wanted and needed dogs were simply unable to check out of their lives for three weeks or a month to get them.

"So we decided—I was going to join them and develop a

program to serve people in their home community. That was the first time it had been formally done in the States." John says the Kamans did not intend to range beyond New England. "I don't think Charlie ever had aspirations for a large organization. He was very interested in what dogs could do for mankind. That was their interest and commitment. And it was an opportunity for them to develop a program that had never been tried before, having only German shepherds. They're still the only organization that uses them exclusively."

John recalls listening to Robbie describe one of the greatest advances in the Fidelco breeding program—the discovery of a brilliant line of shepherds, honed to just the strongest and fittest survivors of the harsh Communist rule in what was then East Germany. He had traveled to England with the Kamans in 1992 when she told the international assembly of dog breeders:

"Circa 1987, some East German dogs were permitted for export to West Germany for hard currency. . . . Fidelco looked long and hard at the potential with great interest and liked what they saw. One such dog made his way to the U.S. and then to Fidelco for breeding at seven and a half years of age, Bodo Grafental. It was like going back thirty to forty years in a genetic time freeze. Our results were so impressive from Bodo in all areas, I went to East Germany to look for a younger male."

In 1987, Robbie and some breeder friends drove through the countryside for eight days, looking at dogs and scouting a large show in Leipzig. Three more dogs were procured. Some of the more desirable traits from the East German imports were overall good health, strong hips, longevity, receptivity to control by a human voice, and a lack of aggression toward other dogs.

Watching the Fidelco line develop, John Byfield has come to have a great deal of respect for the breed and its potential.

"Shepherds are bright. And there is a complexity to many of them. They don't tend to be forgiving, so if you make a mistake it can set you back quite a bit. Psychologically, they find it difficult to undo things. I think you have to be more careful with shepherds than with some of the other breeds."

But patience with shepherds can yield some lasting rewards. Fidelco clients report astonishing feats: Perfect recall of the route to a restaurant visited just once—six months before. An unerring path to a favorite study carrel in a library with hundreds of identical boxes. Mastery of a Manhattan subway route with three tricky changes—and ongoing construction in all stations. "The shepherd has exceptional memory," says John. "It's one of its greatest qualities. They also have very good initiative, the ability to figure things out. They don't have to deliberate and stand there thinking, *What do I do?* They just seem to have an immediate assessment and they're very decisive."

He laughs when it is suggested that he could also be describing Charlie Kaman. "Yes, certainly. Anything he sets his mind to do, he achieves. He's conservative, not flashy, and very practical."

Fund-raising was the initial order of business for Fidelco's formative troika—Robbie, Charlie, and John. "We made a commitment that we had to raise a certain amount of money within a set period before we would change the charter and formalize the program as the Fidelco Guide Dog Foundation," John says. "It was a little iffy."

Setting an initial goal of $150,000, they went to work. "Charlie's friends would put on luncheons and he'd prevail upon some of the corporate types that he knew. We'd go and do presentations. That was the main way we raised money then." Charlie was a strong persuader when it came to the charitable shakedown. The Fidelco shepherds, performing brilliantly in harness, were led out to seal the deal. "We met that first goal very quickly," says John. Besides the roster of outside donors, "the Kaman Corporation gives a very significant donation every year, as do Robbie and Charlie personally. I never knew how much and I didn't inquire. But I believe it was considerable."

Five Fidelco shepherds were trained and placed that first year, 1981, and ten the next. John interviewed all applicants, who were also evaluated by an ophthalmologist and an orthopedist to certify them physically fit to handle a dog. John set about refining and codifying the training system that is still the template for creating a Fidelco guide dog. It begins with a basic commandment: "You have to read the dog. I think that's the most important aspect of all. If you read the dog well, you know what its potential is. You know when you should implement certain things."

Nothing is hurried; lives are in the balance. Training is progressive and relentlessly methodical. "The early training is done in less challenging areas—quiet streets and so forth. Once a dog reaches a certain skill level, then you increase the difficulty factor and expose it to more complicated situations. So you start off working the dog on the leash, teaching it where to walk, the position on the sidewalk, developing its concentration, stopping at curbs automatically, and responding to directional commands."

Despite any natural herding instincts, a dog must learn to account for its appended human burden in every move it makes. "The next stage is to put the harness on the dog and show that when it navigates, it has to include the width and height of a person in addition to its own. The dog learns how to navigate and how much clearance to give." This is done on the street and in obstacle courses on the Fidelco grounds.

The seemingly simple task of going around an object—a mail-box, a propped-open door—may take a month of daily reinforcement to master. "Initially the dog doesn't know why it's doing it. Then it becomes habit. Over time, once the dog has a basic understanding of what its obligation is, you begin the enforcement procedure. You become a little more demonstrative—make sure the dog watches and notices what it's doing, over and over. Then it comes down to trial and error as you let it have more control. You allow the dog to make mistakes and you show what the consequences are. You walk into an object, you stumble and falter, make the dog know that's not a good thing."

Positive reinforcement—praise—is powerful incentive for a breed long accustomed to working in tandem with humans. "When you reach the stage where you allow the dog to make its own judgments, you make it clear: If you do it right, we're going to compliment you. If you make a mistake, we're going to bring it to your attention and show you what you should have done. A bright dog absorbs that quickly."

Mile after mile, day after day, John drilled and tested the Fidelco shepherds. He interviewed applicants for their dogs. He was keenly aware that their new training methods were not one-dog-fits-all.

"The in-community program is probably best as far as the personalized training goes—if you're up to it," he says. "I sit down the first day in a student's home and say, 'What are the things you'd like us to include, what are the places you'd like to go to?' And I make a list. I qualify it by saying, 'Look, I can't give you a timetable on what's going to happen. You've got to learn the fundamentals of handling a dog first. You and the dog have to develop a comfort level.' Then, incrementally, we begin to integrate these activities."

As they learn to navigate at home, in their neighborhoods, schools, churches, and workplaces, John often delivers students home shaken and spent. "It is hard work. There's more strain on an individual with this program because it's more concentrated. There are some people who would benefit from a more structured residential program. They have support from their peers, and there's always someone around at the facility if they have a problem."

It is daunting to find yourself at home with a new dog to care for and a trainer who will be at your door shortly after dawn every morning—in any kind of weather—for three grueling weeks or more. The first lessons involve how to care for the dog, and John stresses that their new partnership must work both ways. "There's a minimum requirement for every dog," he says. "It's not sufficient just to walk the dog around the block. That doesn't satisfy the dog's own emotional and physical needs. Particularly with a young dog—they have to get out and work the dog. That's the way they hone their skills."

Just as a small percentage of dogs prove unsuited for guide work and wash out of the training program. In rare cases, clients decide they cannot continue; the dog is brought back to Fidelco and matched with another client on the waiting list. There is never a shortage of applicants willing to meet the challenge. "The type of person we deal with is basically someone who's more independent, more sure of themselves, more willing to accept the responsibility quickly of caring for the dog. People certainly earn their dogs in this program. There's no easy way to do that. It's almost a sort of tough love."

As they tell their stories in this book, some of John's students will attest to his firm but gentle discipline, as well as a keen set of people skills. He says he learned early that an effective guide dog trainer must also become a canny judge of humankind. "Like assessing the dog, you have to assess the person. What their potential is, what the acceleration of the program should be, what they can handle. Then you develop a very personalized program."

Since this part of the placement process is so critical to a team's success, apprentice instructors are subject to rigorous scrutiny in terms of how they relate to their dogs—as well as their coworkers and clients. "The instructor is probably the most visible part of the organization because he's the direct care provider," John says. "And there is a pretty strong relationship between the instructor and the student. I've always tried to strike a balance where you maintain your professionalism. But you've got to make sure you create a climate where the person is comfortable with you."

Trust the trainer?

"Exactly."

After forty-eight years and thousands of miles training visually impaired people with their dogs, John—like Robbie—sees no reason he should leave off doing what he loves best. After retiring as director of training at Fidelco in 1999, he has worked in the field as an instructor for the foundation, taking dogs to clients and building working teams. So he knew precisely what he was doing when he accepted his new position with Freedom Guide Dogs. "It's fairly physical—there's a lot of walking involved. And you have to be sharp to deal with any situation that arises. But my interest level has always been very high, my health is still stable, and I can still walk a number of hours every day—which I do. I'll continue as long as they need me and I'm able."

Every new client and dog brings challenges and rewards. And there is so much left to do. Public awareness of guide dog users is not what it could be. Out on the job, winning hearts and minds is an ongoing struggle.

> *"No. No you cannot come in here. No dogs. You must go."*
>
> *The hostess at the Chinese restaurant is adamant. And the girl with the guide dog, accompanied by her mother, is mortified. John didn't warn her about this. It's 2009; don't these people know the law?*
>
> *Training with John Byfield and her new dog has gone well for this seventeen-year-old girl in Pennsylvania—so well that he had suggested she and her mother take a break for some shopping and lunch before their afternoon session. She will be going away to college in the fall; her mother is reassured by the safety and independence this animal might give her there.*
>
> *But this is awful—people are staring and making comments. Some customers are chastising the hostess, who is becoming loudly furious. Others support her—who wants a darn dog where you're eating?*
>
> *"You must go—now!" The hostess has summoned her husband, the restaurant owner. And he, too, is adamant. The girl stands her ground, tells him she is not leaving, and calls John Byfield on her cell phone. He is there within minutes, explaining the situation to the restaurant owner and calming the girl. He always gives what he calls the discrimination talk at the end of training—they just hadn't gotten there yet. He tells all his students that things like this will happen, over and over. One can summon the police in a case like this. They must enforce disability laws allowing guide dogs in public places.*
>
> *Seeing the girl's discomfort, John takes over. Normally,*

he might stand by and let his student handle it. But this restaurateur is loud and unpleasant in his refusal of service. When the situation is finally defused and the dog allowed to stay, John turns to the shaken girl with some positive reinforcement:

"Good for you, not just walking away. Always trust yourself. And stand your ground."

John says he did phone the police after the incident and asked them to visit the restaurant owner, who was clearly still angry and unconvinced of his legal requirements. Incidents like this stay with you for a while, he admits. Fortunately, they are counterbalanced by moments of unalloyed joy—fleeting but wonderfully sweet. They are potent enough to have kept him out on the road all these years, grateful for his wearying, challenging, purpose-driven métier.

"When I was working on Long Island, we trained for the city in Flushing, Queens. Since I worked with dogs in London, I was always fascinated by working in the city. Once you get a dog to a certain standard, you see them zipping along the sidewalk, handling it well—it's awe-inspiring to think that a dog is capable of doing that. I still get a thrill each time I see a dog functioning well like that. It's never old hat. Never."

Another 4-H meeting geared to the canine crowd in the basement of the Litchfield County Extension Service. In 1977, there are still plenty of working farms in this northwest corner of Connecticut, and any high school has its complement of cow kids, goat and sheep fanciers, and assorted aggies. Dave Darr is a dog guy; his family has always had shepherd dogs and he has been fostering another of the Kamans' puppies—

his third. It's fun and he's happy to do it, despite all the sodden newspapers and baby gates required. But he has never actually seen a person with a guide dog—until tonight's film about a guide dog trainer. Given the scenery on-screen, it's clear the trainer is working in New York City.

The man and the harnessed dog are doing a smooth, perfectly synced serpentine through a thick crowd, and as the camera pulls back Dave thinks, "Hey, that must be Times Square." As the shot goes wider still, he sees the full scope of what man and dog are contending with: kamikaze traffic across six lanes, blaring taxi horns, pushcarts, news kiosks, street hustlers, baby strollers, and the prone-and-sleeping homeless. The dog is dodging obstacles like a quarter horse in a barrel race. But he makes it look effortless, moving his handler subtly, with almost imperceptible tugs. Oh, man— are they headed into the subway?

Wow. So this is what it's all about. This is what these puppies grow up to do. As the lights come on, Dave feels that something has grabbed him. What the man was doing— that's cool, that's good stuff. That is what he wants to do.

"It hit me and I didn't know what to do with it, where to go," Dave Darr recalls. Seated behind the desk in his capacity as Fidelco's director of student services—he's in charge of clients' training and placement—he could be the blond, fit, fleece-jacketed head of a New England ski resort. He does prefer the outside work—training dogs and students—to the administrative requisites of supervising a staff of seventeen that is pushing hard to train and place a hundred guide dogs each year. Some days, he admits, "I'll just go down to the kennel, grab a dog, and take it for a test walk, just to get back out there."

There were times, during his earliest apprenticeship, doing scut work in the kennels, learning the training procedures in the streets of nearby Windsor, that people assumed he was John Byfield's son. But he had to campaign—assiduously—to join Fidelco's founding family. There was no room or salary for an eager apprentice in those initial months, as the dogs were just being introduced to those rudimentary test-rig kennels.

It would take four years for Dave to secure that dream job. Having met Robbie Kaman in the Fidelco/4-H program, he began petitioning in a series of letters. Was there some way he could come aboard and learn how to do this? Always, the answer was a polite and not entirely discouraging "Not just yet." Dutifully, he kept his job in the men's clothing store where one of his four brothers worked until, finally, he got a phone call from Charlie Kaman. "He said, 'Why don't you come down and we'll talk.' I'd seen him, and met him through the foster program, but I had no idea what type of man he was, or that he had a company on the Fortune 500. He was just part of this lovely couple that did this guide dog work."

Dave was nonplussed when he drove to the Kamans' Farmington home and the gates swung open for him. "Sitting down with him, I realized that he was the head cheese, the big guy," he says of Charlie. "He was interested in what I was about. That was really my first big job interview. I was twenty-two, twenty-three at the time, and I was intimidated." They talked at the kitchen table. The older man's attention was keen, almost piercing, as he peppered Dave with questions about himself. When he was finished, Charlie told him, "I can tell in your eyes that this is something for you. We'll be in touch with you in the next few weeks."

Soon Dave was wielding his own shovel in the Fidelco kennels, with the blessing of his girlfriend, Debbie—now his wife—who had sweetly assured him, "You get that job you want so much or I'll kick your behind." He had satisfied his father's worried queries. Is it a real career? Will it let you support a family?

Dave washed and fed dogs, shoveled snow and anything else necessary, and was grateful that he had found a vocation, rather than a mere job. Knowing that he and Debbie wanted a family, he had been careful to add up the negatives. Placing dogs with clients, he would be away for weeks at a time; if they ran into trouble later, he would have to pack a bag almost immediately and help them work it out. Training dogs in New England, he would see more rain, snow, and sleet than the heartiest mail carrier. The worst weather days could be construed as "good training days," since guide dogs must know how to recognize and navigate black ice and snow drifts. But even as he worked his first dogs through the local streets under John's tutelage, passersby would occasionally voice what he already knew:

"Man, you have a very cool job."

Dave smiles. "Of course, they only say that on beautiful days." Unless he was facing a tough chore, such as retiring a much-loved dog, he can't recall not wanting to come to work. "It's a simple lifestyle, but there's a lot involved. I learn so much from the dogs about behavior. They're trying to tell us something—we're just not smart enough to communicate with them. I think that dogs are better people than we are. They are great judges of character. And they never complain."

He is convinced that dogs employ a superior wisdom when it comes to dealing with disabled humans. As service animals, they are submissive to their handler as the dominant one in the relationship—but they are stubbornly assertive when the boss is in danger. "I first heard the phrase 'intelligent disobedience' from the Kamans," Dave says. "At some point, maybe through the maturity and closeness of the relationship, the dog realizes that it has to assume some responsibility. Where it says, *You know what? I wouldn't cross with that car so close and I'm not going to have you do it either.*" Thus a decisive dog will override a command of "forward"—until the coast is clear.

Shepherds tend to form strong and lasting bonds with humans. By way of illustration, Dave cites a certain female named Nina. She was a fiercely intelligent daughter of the aforementioned Bodo, the finest shepherd dog he has ever known. And she was initially in Dave's string of trainees until John Byfield and Charlie Kaman watched her training in Hartford one day and decided that with those impeccable genes, her greatest contribution would be in the breeding program.

There was also the little matter of Nina's extravagant affection for her trainer. She became so attached to Dave that she scaled the kennel's six-foot chain-link fence several times to keep him in her sights. Since breed dogs live with Fidelco volunteer families between litters, Nina's besotted escape capers secured her a place with her beloved. "Dave," Charlie Kaman told him, "looks like you've got yourself a dog."

These four people working in that drafty test rig with Fidelco's first string of dogs have since changed thousands of lives—including their own. The Kamans, John Byfield, and Dave Darr will appear throughout this narrative, as guide dog recipients unspool their remarkable stories. All four are doers more than talkers. But it is Robbie Kaman—unsalaried, resolutely unimpressed with herself, and able to find a prayer in a puppy's sigh—who can best explain the steadfast, panting heart of a service-oriented dog person. Ask her what draws her here, day after day for two-thirds of her lifetime, and she admits to a shy, almost maternal pride in the intelligent, exuberant animals she sends out into the world. She prefers the simplest pleasures.

"I most enjoy two things—going to puppy classes on Saturdays and watching the progression of litters," she says. "You see them when they go out at eight weeks and in another three weeks, you see them again at puppy class. And on it goes until they come back to us for training. You can tell as they progress whether you've got a group of great dogs or average dogs."

What she loves most is contained in the ephemeral moments she cannot predict or summon; they come once the finished guide dogs have left her care: "When you see a dog that's working well with a graduate. Or you get a letter from one of them, and you see that it's a good fit all around. It's hard to describe. But that's your payoff."

After all this time, there is one aspect of her work that surprised her. It became apparent in the early eighties, shortly after the placements with visually impaired clients began. "You have to be part social worker. You're involved in so many things. . . . " Robbie pauses to hush a barking office dog. "People say we're in the dog business, but we're not. We're in the people business."

CHAPTER TWO

NINA, ZURI, AND
THE FIDELCO WAY

The most important—and the hardest—thing is just trust-ing the dog, just letting go. The first time I took her harness, I said, "Can I have my cane, too?" and they said NO. There were moments that were frustrating at first. But you learn. Zuri got used to me and I got used to her. We've been every-where together—in Greece, Serbia, Hungary. She's a symbol of my independence, my beautiful girl.

—Nina Bektic

How is it that a dog bred in Connecticut from Bavarian stock and a young refugee from a war-torn Balkan nation come to walk and work as one? By what process—part intuitive, part deliberate and careful training—is their extraordinary bond formed?

For Nina Bektic, the extraordinary chain of events lead-ing her to a deep partnership with her guide dog, Zuri, is "very much a love story." Maybe, she jokes, the uncanny matching of her hard-charging personality with a fast-paced, powerful dog is "some kind of crazy positive voodoo." But standing behind Nina and Zuri is a support system of hundreds: Fidelco animal husbandry experts, puppy foster families, veterinarians, trainers, donors, Lions Club fund-raisers, 4-H Club members, and other volunteers.

The wartime backdrop to Nina and Zuri's transatlantic pas de deux may be among the more dramatic of the more than 1,200 Fidelco pairings thus far. But their partnership's main theme—an odyssey from grief, depression, and isolation to independence and trust—resonates strongly throughout the community of guide dog users and their families. Watching the two come together opens an intimate window on the Fidelco process.

Nina

In the midst of a long, bloody, and globally reported conflict, a child rescued from a war zone is always good copy. And so it was in May 1999, when the New York *Daily News* ran a small human-interest feature: CITY DOCS TREAT SERB TEEN'S BRAIN TUMOR.

The story filtered out the confusing sprawl of a long and agonizing civil war in Yugoslavia and focused on the thin, exhausted face of one desperately ill refugee. She arrived as NATO bombs—in a campaign that participating U.S. forces dubbed "Operation Noble Anvil"—pounded Belgrade and surrounding areas in an attempt to dismantle Serbian strongman Slobodan Milošević's military infrastructure, which had been raining terror on the diverse population of Bosnia since 1991. By decade's end, the war had moved south to the long-contested region known as Kosovo. The article began:

A blind Serb teenager, weary and shaken from months of bombing raids near her Belgrade apartment, is recovering from an emergency surgery at Beth Israel Medical Center to save her life.

Nina Bektic and her mother made a harrowing seven and a half hour bus trip out of Yugoslavia last week, carrying medical visas and CAT scans of the brain tumor that grew as doctors treated NATO bombing victims in worse shape than the frightened 14-year-old.

As the girl's weeping mother, Branka Ljubicic, explained to the reporter through a translator, it all seemed hideously unfair. The NATO bombing of Belgrade, an attempt to end what became known as the Kosovo War, was the second conflict to have an impact on her daughter's young life. Six years earlier, Nina, her mother, and her grandmother had fled escalating hostilities in the city of Sarajevo, where their Christian Serbian family had lived for centuries.

"When it got bad in Sarajevo, you just couldn't leave the house," Nina recalls now. She is speaking in her new home, a sunny two-bedroom rental apartment in Westchester County, New York, that overlooks the far banks of the Hudson River. At twenty-five, she is petite and dark-haired, a new wife and mother tender as a just-bloomed snowdrop—unless you are fool enough to deny her rights as a person with a disability.

Her small family has not lived here long—there are still a few boxes to unpack. Nina moves easily around the apartment's comfortable rooms with the determined grace of the expertly blind. Yet as she talks about her childhood home, the confident woman curls more compactly on the sofa and her voice, still lightly accented, drops a level. Reflexively, she reaches to stroke her guide dog, Zuri, who is looking keenly at her.

"Zuri always knows when I'm stressed out," she says. "She is my eyes, my heart, my love." The big dog puts her head on her paws, and heaves a deep canine sigh as Nina continues her narrative.

"In Sarajevo, people were getting killed left and right. They disappeared. There were concentration camps." She stops, and resorts to a phrase that she tosses often over the most excruciating memories that cannot, should not, be unveiled: "It was . . . really tough."

She was not quite eight when her mother made the decision to try to get all three of them out of harm's way. Long separated from Nina's Muslim father, Branka had been supporting her mother and daughter with a good management position at the city's Holiday Inn. But the situation was deteriorating as the city's roiling ethnic factions—Serbs, Croats, Muslims—squared off beneath the genocidal terrors of Milošević's brutal incursions. Even for a first grader like Nina, negotiating the city's severely altered daily life called for a new set of age-inappropriate vocabulary words: murder, rape, torture.

"We just decided we couldn't do it anymore," Nina says. "We had to leave because we were three women all by ourselves. There were a lot of threatening phone calls, telling us that our end was near. It got very tense—we had no male in the house to protect us." Their apartment had become a fortress, with furniture pushed up against the front door and a doomsday plan formulated by her grandmother, Jagoda Cortula, a resilient woman who had lost her father and all siblings but one in World War II.

"My grandma put an ax right next to the door. If anybody broke through to attack us—which is what they were threatening over the phone—her plan was to stand there and fight while Mami jumped with me through the window. Because the worst thing that can happen to a person is to get raped. And that was mostly what was happening—before they would murder you. We lived on the eighth floor, so we would really be jumping to our deaths. But it was better than torture. It was very tough, psychologically, on these two women."

Finally, in April 1992, Branka secured passage on a cargo plane headed south, to Belgrade. Nina cried for her dolls left behind and took along one beloved comfort toy, a stuffed monkey named Dimitri that her mother had brought back from a business trip to Greece. They made it through a labyrinth of barricades to the plane, which was jammed with tense refugees and their bundles, yet oddly silent.

"Everyone was so afraid. We were all sitting on the floor where normally the merchandise goes. I was so tiny but I remember. Everybody was just curled up next to each other. My mother says it was the last cargo plane out of Sarajevo during the conflict."

They got out as the city's unspeakable agony, now remembered as the Siege of Sarajevo, was just beginning. In the longest siege of a capital city in modern history, massive shelling by an estimated 18,000 rebel Serb forces outside the city would destroy in excess of 35,000 buildings. Over nearly four years, more than 10,000 citizens stranded in the surrounded city would perish from bombs, sniper bullets, hunger, lack of medical care, and cold. An estimated 1,500 of the dead were children.

Once the trio resettled as refugees in Belgrade, Branka took any and all work available, in a supermarket, a hamburger grill, and a kiosk selling cigarettes and coffee. The smallest domestic errands became exercises in the absurd. Wartime inflation was so wild and supplies so short that in the supermarket where Branka worked, Nina recalls, "the value of money was constantly dropping, zeros were added, they couldn't even punch in so many. They had to write more zeroes on the cash register. For bread it was like two billion dinars."

Occasionally, Branka brought home a few precious eggs on credit against her future wages, trying to conceal them from neighbors who loudly denounced the refugees as greedy and grasping. Paranoia snapped in the wind between apartment buildings like the worn, dispirited clothing on the city's wash lines. Privation bred poisonous thoughts amid neighbors. "We were lucky that Mami worked in a store," Nina says. "She worked very hard for everything, but we were never hungry. But there were families that would be standing in line for hours to get a liter of oil. At that point, people become very vicious and envious."

Amid the grating tensions, Nina went to school and burrowed into its comforting routines. She earned straight A's and loved reading and sports, especially tennis. "I was a school freak—you might call me a nerd. I just loved it." But at nearly fourteen, something began clouding her vision. She realized how poor her sight had become when the geography teacher called her to a large map of Serbia during a test and asked her to point out the Danube. "It's one of the biggest rivers in Europe, and I couldn't see it." She stood silent in front of the class, mortified as the surprised teacher gave her star pupil a score of 1, the equivalent of an F. At home, Nina told her mother she was frightened at how little she could see.

The first doctor informed Branka that Nina was just another wily eighth grader—a typical adolescent faking to get out of school. "Liar!" she snapped at him, and led her child away. The second doctor saw the problem at once: seriously atrophied optic nerves and life-threatening intracranial pressure from a growing tumor that was causing fluid to back up at the front of Nina's skull. On October 9, 1998, Nina's waist-length hair was shaved on one side for emergency surgery.

"They installed a shunt to divert fluid that was building up because of the tumor and causing hydrocephaly, making my forehead swell. They thought the repair would last. Then in January the pump stopped working. And my vision started totally going."

Belgrade medicine could offer her no more. Branka, normally a bubbly, outgoing presence in the coffee kiosk, had grown so withdrawn that a frequent customer asked her what was wrong. "And luckily," says Nina, "she opened up." On hearing of Nina's condition, the woman offered the help of her daughter, a doctor in Chicago. But she would need to see some medical records. "My mother had to get the scans onto little slides, which cost more than her whole salary for months. But somehow she got it done in February and they were sent to New York. The lady's daughter had contacted Dr. Fred Epstein at Beth Israel. And he was willing to view the slides."

Dr. Epstein, who has since died, was a pediatric neurosurgeon at Beth Israel Medical Center in New York. Once Branka sent an additional MRI confirming the failed shunt and grim prognosis, Dr. Epstein informed her that he could arrange for emergency treatment through a humanitarian program at the hospital called Save One Child.

It was a flare of hope. But in March, as Branka poured frantic energy into arranging the trip, the NATO bombing of Belgrade began. In their sparsely furnished apartment, barely more than a ten-foot-by-ten-foot cubby partitioned from the bathroom of an old office building, Nina and her mother and grandmother huddled during the fusillades on their shared bed—a plywood sleeping platform covered with discarded sofa cushions. The bomber aircraft screamed in from bases in Italy and from the decks of the carrier USS *Theodore Roosevelt* anchored in the Adriatic Sea. Building foundations shook with the percussive force of incoming Tomahawk cruise missiles and cluster bombs.

Along with their parents, schoolchildren learned quickly to distinguish ordnance sounds and features. In the hopes of avoiding the infamous "collateral damage" of dead civilians, the U.S. forces turned to new technologies that would be more reliable in locking onto only military targets. But the citizens of Belgrade didn't get that Pentagon briefing, Nina says. And the sophisticated weaponry blasting the city apart looked as deadly as any other from the ground.

"The Tomahawk is a self-leading, or smart, bomb, which means that it locates its own target," Nina says. "Every night at seven or so, the sirens would go off that the bombing is starting. In the beginning, people were going into shelters, but after a week or so of bombing raids people would just go to bed. Because there's not much you can control."

The surreal became the commonplace; Branka stepped out of the building one day to see a smart bomb pass by on its deadly mission "just like a person walking down the street," Nina recalls. Daily, before the sirens sent them indoors, children rushed to collect what they knew as the locators—small signal-emitting devices dropped to help guide incoming missiles. The children piled the locators into less populated areas. "Nobody was organized," Nina says, "but people had to do something. When the power plants would shut down from sabotage, people would go outside the buildings and collect wood and cook, make big pots of bean soup. Everybody did what we could to survive."

Adults burned car tires in the streets, in vain hopes that the fumes would confuse the incoming bomb sensors. The children continued their ghastly hide-and-seek with locators, but Nina had become too ill to participate in this apocalyptic playtime. "I could smell the burning rubber of the tires. But that time is so much like in a fog. It was so painful that half of the things blacked out in my mind."

The apartment was darkened by blankets nailed up to shield the women from flying shards of window glass—darker still for Nina, who grew steadily worse. The fluid buildup was causing crushing headaches amplified by the nightly explosions. Branka knew she had no time to lose. Only one border—that with Hungary—was left open. Finally, with a written guarantee from Dr. Epstein to satisfy border officials, they made it out of Yugoslavia by bus to the American Embassy in Budapest on the fifty-fifth day of the bombing. Dimitri the stuffed monkey went along.

Nina says the worst part was not the danger and anxiety of the journey; their escape was also an excruciating act of abandonment. "We left my grandma there. She could not get exit papers. There are no words to explain it to you. It was horrific." Blanka's choice was the life of her child—or the possible loss of her own mother, stalwart but alone amid the bombs. Throughout the leave-taking and the journey to New York, says Nina, "we could never stop crying."

On May 24, the endoscopic surgery at Beth Israel Institute for Neurology and Neurosurgery was successful in relieving the blockage; the tumor was found to be benign and, owing to its difficult position, it was left intact. For a few days, Nina's vision seemed to improve. But the war's delay had caused too much irreversible damage. Her sight flickered out again, and could not be restored. Doctors pronounced Nina Bektic, fourteen, legally blind.

At the time, she was not ready to accept the truth she can speak of evenly, almost clinically, now. "Today, I have eyesight of approximately five percent in my right eye and one percent in my left, which is not much," she says. "But it's something. It's very dark, cloudy. If a hand passes by my face, a picture will arrive a couple of seconds later. I can see the shadow and movement."

Confronted with her disability in a huge foreign city, with very little English at her command, Nina says she "literally turned my face to the wall for about three months." She and her mother were living at Ronald McDonald House in Manhattan while she attended an English as a Second Language program for immigrant children at Liberty High School and underwent rehabilitation treatment. With teachers from the Lighthouse for the Blind, she began learning cane mobility skills to navigate the city. And amid another set of refugees—McDonald House families uprooted by catastrophic illness—she found an ally against despair:

"We met a couple from Greece whose son was very ill. Kostas. He was like my brother. He had a tumor and a variety of related conditions. We had a plan that when both of us got well we would go on with our lives, take family vacations, be next to each other. We were really close. He was in his early twenties. He died right after his birthday, on the exact anniversary of the bombing raids back in my country, March 24."

For a few moments, she is unable to go on.

"It was really tough."

Looming beyond her grief was the approaching expiration of their visa. It had been granted at the American embassy in

Budapest on humanitarian grounds with an eighteen-month limit. And there was not much left in Belgrade or Sarajevo for anyone, let alone a newly disabled teenager. "I dreaded going back home," she says, "because of the lack of any possibility for my education or a career."

Kostas's parents, having returned to Greece, offered to sponsor Nina and Branka there. In Athens, through the intercession of a Greek journalist who had reported from Kosovo, Nina was introduced to people connected with the American embassy, including Elizabeth Burns, wife of the then–U.S. ambassador to Greece, R. Nicholas Burns. They helped her get a scholarship for a private American high school in Athens.

She began her new life's trajectory at the school in February 2001. Using her cane, she made her way along the ancient, curving Athenian streets with a quiet resolution she kept to herself. "I could use a cane okay, but it was slow. And I was always in a big hurry. I had a plan."

Zuri

The female puppy assigned Fidelco ID #51336 was born on May 27, 2002, a feisty, robust member of a litter of eight whelped by Wonie (pronounced Vahnee), a breeding German shepherd imported from Bavaria. The puppies' handsome, outgoing sire, Troy, had become something of a local celebrity, representing Fidelco at public functions and fund-raisers. Throughout his breeding career, he fathered very fine puppies, Robbie Kaman recalls—healthy, intelligent, good tempered, and well suited to the guide dog's mission.

Little miss #51336 rolled, nipped, and nursed with her siblings in Fidelco's pine-shaded puppy house, duly endured her shots and weaning, and chowed down on a custom diet of raw meats frozen and shipped by Fidelco's longtime supplier, Robert Abady Dog Foods of Poughkeepsie, New York. Until she found Abady's breed-specific raw meat blends and dry food, Robbie Kaman had ground, chopped, and mixed tons of her own blend, for hundreds of dogs.

On July 20, Charlene and Paul Picard of Colchester, Connecticut, collected the pup they would raise for about a year and a half in their home, along with a supply of food and a snappy red vest that would identify her as a service dog in training. "We don't have children, and we were looking for a way to give back . . . something," says Charlene. She and Paul fostered their first Fidelco puppy, Logan, in 1993, and after six more, they have not looked back. Troy, retired from his breeding duties, now lives with the Picards, along with his daughter Inga, who is in Fidelco's breeding program, and the latest foster puppy, Trekker.

"I went to the puppy classes of all Troy's offspring," confesses Charlene, who is also involved in Fidelco fund-raising and online chat groups with other foster families. "Does that make me obsessed?"

The citizens of Colchester are used to seeing the Picards and their puppies all over town—in the post office, the banks, the big-box stores—as they fulfill the fosters' key assignment of exposing puppies to every aspect of the human world possible. By the time the couple arrived in Bloomfield to pick up female #51336, they had little need of the fat instruction packet handed to first-time foster families.

The Picards were well aware that Fidelco dogs are named in alphabetical cycles. And their newest puppy was from a group of litters identified as Z-19. This meant that her name would begin with a Z, and this was the nineteenth time since 1960 that the kennel's litters had cycled through the alphabet. Foster families must choose easily pronounced names beginning with their assigned letter, of one or two syllables.

Browsing an online baby-naming site, Charlene says she quickly found a fitting Z name. "Zuri. It's an African word for 'beautiful.'" And Zuri was surely that—big-boned but lithe, with a dark muzzle and expressive brown eyes set against a lighter face. "She was a very happy little girl," Charlene recalls. Zuri stole and cheerily mutilated socks until she learned to surrender them for food treats, got expansively carsick for the first four months, and bounced confidently toward every new experience the Picards provided for her—with the notable exception of a visit to the Harvest Fair in Hebron, Connecticut.

On a busy Friday night at the fair, she was anxious to explore, weaving through the crowds in her red Fidelco vest, even gently nudging some passersby to clear the way for the couple. But on a return visit Sunday morning, the intrepid pup froze on a visit to the animal barns as a teenager leading a lumbering cow approached. Zuri's hackles rose. She tried to back away. Charlene saw a teaching experience.

"I brought her to where I could give her treats as the cow and the girl passed by. Then I brought her to where she could sit next to me and get treats while we watched another girl bathe a cow about fifty feet away and she was much more comfortable with that. About two months later, I took Zuri for a walk in West Hartford Center when the 'Cow Parade'—dozens of brilliantly painted fiberglass cows—came to town."

Zuri's hackles shot up at the first gaudy life-sized statue. Charlene patted the cow, and coaxed the dog to sniff and explore. They continued down the line of cows until, at last, Zuri was calm and even curious. It was the Fidelco way: gentle, incremental introduction to all aspects of the wider world—a method reinforced by mandatory puppy classes every other Saturday at the foundation's training center in Bloomfield. Zuri's rambunctious preschool is still in session there with a time-tested curriculum of work and play.

"Let's have all T puppies in the outdoor pen, please!"

Grouped by age for each of the day's five sessions, the puppies tumble out of vans and station wagons with their doting fosters: silver-haired seniors in down vests and hiking shoes, teenagers in 4-H and Jonas Brothers T-shirts, middle-aged empty nesters like Tom and Patty Adams from Stonington, Connecticut, here today with their eighth Fidelco puppy. Some weekends, the Adamses take their pups to Mystic Seaport, which, Tom says, "has got it all—crowds, strollers, wheelchairs, kids, Frisbee players, picnickers—the full complement of distractions."

The foster folk are all busy, filling and adjusting little pouches of dog training treats on their belts, slipping bridle-like Gentle Leader collars onto their dogs that keep heads up and focused without yanking or discomfort. During a brief romp in an outdoor pen to help socialize the dogs—and burn off excess puppy energy—their handlers lean against the chain-link fence, swapping stories like any playground parents:

"We're a bit too possessive with our toys."

"He ate half a meatloaf before we could catch him."

"Tell her 'Leave it!' and she'll do just the opposite."

"Thank heaven, he's stopped upchucking in the car."

Always leashed and often vested in public to identify them as service dogs in training, Fidelco pups go everywhere

their families go—to picnics, reunions, 4-H and PTA meet-
ings, supermarkets, libraries, shopping malls, playgrounds,
beaches, and parks. Most travel well; others must adjust.
Thus car sickness remedies—Robbie Kaman often coun-
sels fosters to have a chew toy to keep a pup's mind off its
misery—are avidly discussed as the group files into a vast
indoor training room.

"Shall we begin?"

Foster Program Director Sue Holt-Brown and her two
assistants, Sally Keating and Laura Boogaert, preside over
what initially looks like barely contained chaos. But in short
order, puppies are going through their training exercises,
learning to sit and stay, to heel, to come as their names are
called, to find a handler calling them from a hiding place.

"Does anybody have a vacuum cleaner issue?"

A few hands go up. As the leashed puppies circle the
room with their handlers, a vacuum is set aroar. Some dogs
pass by blithely; those that shy from the racket are encour-
aged to move closer and nose around. Amid the exercises,
Pam Bock, a dog trainer from Massachussetts here with
Ida, her twenty-seventh foster pup, hops into a motorized
wheelchair donated for puppy training. She weaves through
the action with an added distraction—a lively boxer seated
in her lap. Pam has also adopted Aspen, a retired Fidelco
breed dog, and cares for Aspen's son Dimitri, who is carry-
ing on the line as a stud.

Today, Pam has also brought along another dog she has
been boarding to mingle with the shepherd pups. It is the
largest and most delusional Great Dane anyone here has
ever seen. Anytime Pam sits down, the mammoth dog tries
to sit in her lap.

Watching the proceedings, as she has every weekend for decades, is Robbie Kaman. Seated off to the side, she is keeping a close eye on gait, confirmation, attention span, and temperament. "We need a very social dog," she explains as handlers trade dogs and take turns working them. "A lot of fosters take them to church, to work, out shopping, the library. In this state, if you are raising a service dog you can pretty much take it anyplace you can take a guide dog. Some restaurants are a little touchy about it. We've had some people that have taken them on vacation on planes, trains. Hotels, too. They get introduced—hopefully—to everything they will be confronted with once they start to work."

All fosters feel free to call Sue or Robbie, anytime, with any issue. Robbie has diagnosed itchy belly rashes on digital photos sent via e-mail and dispensed advice on skunk-sprayed coats, Lyme-carrying ticks, sore paws, and chewing manias. Just now she has been eyeing a puppy seated far across the large room. Quietly, she asks that it be brought to her. And gently, she opens the dog's mouth.

"Just as I thought. She's got a bit of an overbite."

Pam is stunned. "How could you even see that at such a distance?"

The puppy's teenage handler is visibly concerned. "Can she still be a guide dog?"

Robbie reassures the girl: "Of course. She's still got better teeth than I have."

Behind her, Sue Holt-Brown is headed toward a rangy, long-haired shepherd as she manipulates a big, child-sized doll, its pink arms thrust toward the dog's face. The puppy stands calmly as the fat plastic hands tousle its ears.

"Good boy! What a very good boy!"

Charlene Picard cries every time she returns a puppy to the Fidelco kennels for its guide dog training, which will last from six to eight months, depending on the animal. And it was tougher than usual to hand over the leash with the impish, sweet-tempered Zuri.

Leaving a cushy foster home for boot camp in the kennel can be stressful to young dogs, too. Trainers help ease the transition with playtimes, and returning dogs are housed in pairs, for companionship. Zuri managed her kennel transition without difficulty. Dave Darr remembers her as a quick-learning trainee with a strong, rapid pace. Monday through Friday, she hopped into her crate in a van with several other dogs in Dave's string of canine cadets for transport to a progression of training grounds in a small town (nearby Windsor), a more congested suburb (West Hartford), and finally crowded urban settings (Hartford, Boston, New York City). He says that her potential was evaluated in a standard way.

"The first two weeks is done right here at Fidelco. We do the basics and then it's time to take the dog into the street, usually in Windsor. We have the dog on a leash, but we're not really asking it for too much. We'll just observe the dog, make sure it's stable, not reactive to traffic or any other outside influence. We need to see that it's motivated, highly interested in what we're doing and what's around. That's all we're looking for."

There are, of course, some less-than-ideal candidates—dogs who cannot overcome their instincts to chase every squirrel and chipmunk, who aren't companionable, energetic, or smart enough for guide work but may make a fine police scent dog or a pet. All but one of Zuri's littermates made the cut. And she was an especially quick study—curious, energetic, and ready for initial street training. Every day, in all weather, they walked the quiet byways of Windsor.

"After three weeks comes the real skill set," says Dave. "Everything from walking straight lines to speed control—not going too fast yet showing some degree of initiative. They learn curb stops, halting automatically at up and down curbs until the handler finds the edge with a foot as a blind person might and gives the command to go forward. And that's a lot." Just walking in straight lines on a man-made walkway—a sidewalk or road—has to be learned. And as apprentice trainers find out quickly, "going off a designated path is very natural for dogs. They want to sniff and explore all the little doggie bulletin boards along the way— fire hydrants, posts, stop signs. It's instinctive for them to do it. And all of a sudden they can't."

The Fidelco system of training as designed by John Byfield teaches the necessary skills with a long, careful series of small steps reinforced by praise. During subsequent years when Dave Darr supervised the training department, handlers also rewarded learned behavior with small dog treats from a pouch on the trainer's belt. A reassuring sound—an aural marker—from a clicker at the instant of the desired behavior is another positive reinforcement. Treats and clicker are phased out once the dog has mastered a task. Despite these modifications, Dave insists, a warm and positive training experience is still paramount—along with the proper reading of the dog.

"You do get a lot of praise and love from your handler—if the dog wants that. With some dogs, it's *Just tell me I'm good, that's all I need from you. All I want to do is go.* It's up to the handler to figure that out. Some dogs don't want to be fondled. You figure out what that dog wants and that's what it's going to get."

Once you learn your dog, the dog can learn its job—including the basic and critical task of leading a visually impaired person across a street. "First we have to teach the dog to stop on a verbal command," Dave explains. "Then we teach it to stop at the curb. It's what we call a backward chaining of behavior. You start at the curb, and tell the dog it's a great place to be, a place where you'll get a reward. Boy, you're good. Back up a step, then step up to the curb. Good girl! Feed. Back up two, three steps, do it again."

Zuri mastered curbs in Windsor, both up and down. And as the weeks went by, the intensity increased. The logoed white Fidelco vans donated by various area Lions Clubs took her to an escalating series of challenges with Dave and other trainers.

"You can say, 'Okay, the dog knows curbs.' But the dog needs to know curbs in all types of environments. That's what we call generalizing the behavior. Instead of Windsor, it's going to be in West Hartford, and we have to make sure the dog stops at those curbs as well. Then we go into the downtown business district in Hartford, where there's more going on, more congestion, more dogs. Everything is ramped up. Once we do this in several locations, you can pretty much say the dog knows curbs."

In like manner, Zuri learned the more complex requisites: how to gently, almost imperceptibly, move her handler around objects—mailboxes, lampposts—and back to the center of a sidewalk, how to steer him away from objects overhead, such as a low-hanging tree branch. Obstacles are difficult: though they see things at a different level and without the cognition of humans, dogs must perceive the difference between a hole and a patch of ice as something to be avoided. They learn what is expected in a painstaking series of small increments that may take two to three weeks of repetition. Again, Dave says, success depends on a trainer reading the dog.

"Occasionally, when the dog is overwhelmed by what we're teaching it, we might back off of our expectations. It may show signs it doesn't really want to do the work anymore—maybe with heavy breathing or panting, or maybe it seems distracted. We consider that a fault of ours for not reading the dog properly. So it's quitting time. We'll try it again the next day or try a different location. Maybe we'll even back off doing obstacles for a while."

While her fellow trainees took turns going through their paces, Zuri dozed in the van with the other crated dogs. The vans are parked on the top floor of an accommodating parking garage in downtown Hartford. On trips to learn extreme urban navigation, from subways to Times Square, they park atop Manhattan's bustling Port Authority bus terminal. It's a workable quid pro quo: a dozen or so full-grown German shepherds in wide open vans can be a reassuring presence in an urban parking facility. The dogs have shade, air circulation, and companionship during the long training days that may put eight to ten miles on a trainer working a string of six to eight dogs.

As Zuri took her turns in the Hartford streets, she learned how to guide onto escalators and elevators, board a bus and find her handler a seat, retrieve a dropped object, and—perhaps the hardest task—how to negotiate a crowd. Spring warmed toward the summer of 2004 when Charlene Picard got a long-awaited phone call from Fidelco.

Finally, the day had come: Zuri's final "blindfold walk." Her handler Jeff Mann would put on a blindfold and work her through a busy lunchtime crowd in the state capital, with Dave Darr a few steps behind them assessing her performance along the way. Once the walk was finished, there would be an opportunity for the foster family to visit with Zuri before she was placed in service. Camera in hand, Charlene stood anxiously in front of the designated McDonald's, unseen by Zuri, who headed out to face her challenges.

Zuri is in harness beside Jeff, who adjusts the snug black blindfold so that he can see nothing at all. And at a word from Dave, who will be calling out a route bristling with challenges, they're off, down in the elevator, out of the garage, and merging onto a narrow sidewalk with the thickening lunchtime crowd, around parking meters, lampposts, strollers. Their first crossing: a congested two-way, six-lane street. Down curb, stop. Jeff feels and hears the whoosh of traffic just a few feet away. Zuri gets the command, "forward," but does not leave the curb until she turns her head to check traffic that might turn into their path. Up curb, traffic island, down curb, cross.

On to Main Street, where Dave is scouting for some tricky crowd work. He sends them into it: outdoor cafés, awning supports, steam vents, grates, open cellar doorways, newspaper boxes.

Now find a door on the left. A foyer. What's that smell? A thronged food court: people moving in all directions, kiosks, trash cans, tables, and chairs. The team moves smoothly as admiring diners let them pass.

More turns and now—find escalator down. Get Jeff on and off. Now through a revolving door. They're outside, crossing another four-lane, up three flights of stairs outdoors to Constitution Plaza. Right to the Travelers Insurance building, then a wicked outdoor challenge: a thirty-foot-wide set of stairs with no railings. Just past it, they face a shorter flight with differently spaced steps, plus a sudden down curb.

Right on Arch Street, to Zuri's next trial of keen judgment: a crossing where three different streams of traffic can turn in on Jeff. The dog's head swivels to check them all. They're across. Zuri is brisk and confident and on it goes: a perilously angled crosswalk that must take them across six lanes, then a series of bus shelters and a few more four-lane crossings. And finally, the parking garage.

Sally Keating, then Fidelco's foster program director, signaled to Charlene that she could see Zuri approaching the end of her walk. Dave Darr nodded to her; Zuri had made the grade. Recalling the moment, Charlene says, "When you give them up for training, you miss them all, but the Hartford walk is a reminder of why you did it. That day with Zuri, the minute they came through the crowd, the sight of her in harness, her ears up, working through the people, moving so steadily, with such purpose . . . Your heart stops. This is what we work for. No, I haven't got a photo of Zuri at that moment. I was crying too hard to focus."

She did get a posed victory snapshot of Zuri and Jeff, after she and the dog enjoyed a slobbery and wild reunion. In fact, these have proved such memorable lovefests that foster goodbyes are now done at Fidelco. Trainers sharpening their finished guide dogs in Hartford after these meetings realized that some of them were distracted by looking for their fosters on subsequent trips.

Zuri returned to the kennels fit and ready for service, and soon after, John Byfield had a match in mind for her. On

August 23, 2004, he drove the dog to Cambridge, Massachusetts, where she was placed with a Harvard Law School student who had previously tried another, residential guide dog school and quit after a week. In the end, Fidelco wasn't for her, either.

"Zuri was a bit too much dog for her" is Dave Darr's assessment of why the woman called just weeks later to say that she was too overwhelmed with her academic load to work with and care for a dog. John Byfield, who had trained the woman with Zuri in Boston, feels it was a cultural issue as well. The student was from a Central Asian nation that had no cultural referents for such human/animal partnerships.

Zuri was back in the kennel. But someone else was waiting.

The Match

"Moderate cane mobility," Dave Darr was thinking to himself as he watched Nina Bektic approach the agreed-upon meeting place on the campus of Bard College in Annandale-on-Hudson, New York, where she was a sophomore. It was a chill November day in 2004, approaching Thanksgiving. Nina was at Bard on a full scholarship that was awarded after she graduated from the Athens high school at the top of her class with some college-level course work and an impeccable 4.33 average.

Her Fidelco application suggested that she would make the fullest use of a service dog. But Dave admits he had no inkling just how determined Nina Bektic would prove to be. Even her search for the right guide dog school had a set of firm prerequisites. "I had wanted a dog for a long time," Nina says. "That was always my plan. I knew I could go only so far in my life without one. Once I felt settled at Bard, I went online and researched everything going. I already had an offer from another guide dog school. But what I liked about Fidelco is that they actually come to you—they train wherever you are."

She had no intention of disrupting her studies to attend a residential program for a month. And she had a very definite vision of the dog she hoped would change her life. "I love German shepherds. No other school could assure me that I was going to have a shepherd."

The third and decisive factor foreshadowed Nina's future as a human rights activist. At the time, Fidelco's executive director was George Salpietro, who used a dog himself and was the nation's first blind director of a guide dog school. "It made the difference for me," Nina says. "If you're promoting independence for a blind person—not just in movement but in every aspect of life—then you should have blind employees in your organization who have been given opportunities to excel. So I contacted them, sent in my application, and everything went smoothly."

Eric Gardell, then an apprentice trainer, accompanied Dave Darr to Bard to learn how to interview an applicant. The discussion did not focus much on Nina's past—they would only learn the details of her harrowing childhood later. Instead they concentrated on how she envisioned her future. As Dave recalls, "This was a young lady who's obviously made something of herself already, in pursuing higher education. It seemed like she was going places. A go-getter personality like that is the best match with one of our shepherds because those dogs are the same way: *What's up, let's go, let's work.*"

Then the engaging Ms. Bektic threw them a curve. Besides using the dog to get around campus and on frequent trips to Manhattan, Nina planned to study abroad and travel the following semester—just two months away. She was enrolled in a graduate-level program in international relations. In Budapest.

And there would be more travel: after her studies she would spend the summer with her mother and grandmother, who were living back in postwar Serbia.

She realized it was a tall order on short notice. But . . . could they give her a dog capable of international travel—planes, trains, and ancient, winding cobblestone streets? It would have to be a fast dog—she was always in a hurry. And a patient, well-mannered dog—there were classes, seminars, and meetings to sit through. And oh yes—she was also working on founding an advocacy group, which she was calling Visible/Invisible Disabilities Awareness Program (VIDAP). Outmoded, underserving disability laws needed to be changed and enforced in America. There was virtually no advocacy or services for people like herself in Serbia, and she intended to change that as well. She envisioned public speaking, legislative lobbying, more travel. . . . Nina Bektic was clearly an applicant the guide dog community identifies as a "high level" user.

"When Dave left," she says, "I knew I had a dog."

He says there was no voodoo in making the match, just sound logic. "I was working Zuri, and I thought this dog could do it. Knowing the foster and her dedication, I knew that the dog had a good background. As far as socialization goes, Charlene is really diligent about getting a puppy out to see the human world—so it should not be a problem wherever this gal tends to go."

Dave and Eric repaired to Bloomfield to design an intensive campaign that would tailor Zuri's skills to Nina's needs. They drove Zuri to Bard, where Nina met them in the lounge of her dorm. Zuri was curious; she nosed around. For Nina, the first touch was reassuring: a warm nose, strong shoulders, a thick coat. Despite detailed instructions on how to care for a dog— how to feed and water her, put on a harness, take the dog out to relieve herself—Nina was nervous. Yet she pressed to keep Zuri in the dorm right away. Dave says he was no match for her insistence. "I gave her the dog the first night, only because she wanted it. She said, 'You're not taking my baby.' And that was her baby right from the beginning."

This is not to say their first night together was a breeze. "I was taking her out every ten minutes," Nina admits, laughing. "Now that I think about it, I was so dumb. It was too funny. I'd never had a dog. I was changing her water every half an hour. It was very cute. She didn't cry for Dave or for being in a strange place at all. They had this little bell they attached so that I could locate her. After a while I said, 'You sound like a sheep.' So I got rid of her bell. We bonded really quick."

The intensive, compressed training was grueling for everyone; Dave and Eric commuted daily from Connecticut to Bard, and for city and travel specifics, they took Nina and Zuri into Manhattan, onto buses and subways, through the most complex intersections. So that the cobbled streets of eastern Europe would not disorient the dog, they went to Boston, where Dave knew he could find equivalents.

Over Christmas break from Bard, Nina checked into the Marriott near Fidelco's Bloomfield campus for more training over the holiday. She and Zuri had Christmas with Fidelco staffers and their families. She remembers it as a happy, hopeful time. But even the most motivated students can hit a wall.

"We were in front of a building and I had to get Zuri to turn right and find the stairs. She wouldn't do it. And I took her leash and put my hand out and said, 'Here, Dave, I can't do it.' He told me, 'If I take that leash now, you're not going to have Zuri.' He didn't let me give up. And he taught me a really good lesson. You've got to work with the dog—and it's one hundred percent cooperation."

She says she may have had moments of doubting her own strength, but never the dog's. And she continues to be astonished by the depth of Zuri's ability. "I don't trust easily. The war and the life circumstances made me into a person who does try to do a little bit of a judgment before I have faith in things. But she really won my heart right away. With every new thing she did, I was always in disbelief, like, 'Wow, this is incredible.' She showed me, *Hey, I know what I'm doing.*"

And as training progressed, Dave was more convinced they were a good match. "I never had to suggest Nina slow down because I knew that the dog was capable of doing it. And I thought, 'I'm not going to stop her. She's going to do what she intends regardless, so I've got to tailor her a dog that's capable of rolling with the punches.'"

They made their deadline. Zuri settled on the floor compactly, as she had been taught, and napped as their jet screamed across the ocean, headed for Budapest. They settled into academic life in the old city, navigating classrooms, cafés, and cobblestones. Following the school term, Zuri and Nina headed for Belgrade, where Branka and her mother waited at the airport to meet the newest female in their tight, reunited clan. It was a sight to stop traffic in the busy concourse. Guide dogs were virtually unknown in Serbia. What was this big, harnessed creature, surrounded by three happily weeping women?

"Zuri loves my mom, but she literally adores my grandma," Nina says. "The second time we went to Belgrade, Zuri recognized Grandma and she sped up. And when she got to Grandma, she jumped on her and kept on licking her. People at the airport were yelling: 'Oh, my God, the big bad wolf is eating the grandma!'"

The afternoon sun has backlit Zuri, who has been dozing

lightly as her story is told. Nina says that there has been a very rough patch in their life together. In 2008, Zuri had her own health crisis, a serious autoimmune disorder that required surgery and a painful recovery. Tears well and trickle down Nina's cheeks as she begins to describe it. She brushes them away and continues. "I have felt a lot of different kinds of pain. And I have been very afraid in my life. But the thought of losing her—that was unbearable." She says that across the ocean, her grandmother cried for days until the dog was out of danger.

Nina's bond with the dog is so close now, as natural as walking and breathing, that she has had some uncanny moments. She and Zuri are connected in ways she can't begin to explain.

Nina is unusually exhausted after a workday, half dozing on her bed. Her fiancé, Jose Marrero, is still at work but . . . what's happening?

"Zuri! Zuri, off!"

Her well-behaved girl has leaped onto the bed—something Fidelco dogs are trained never to do. And until this moment, Zuri never has disobeyed that edict. She is noisily vocal—also unusual. Her muzzle gently but persistently nudges Nina's stomach.

"What's wrong with you? Are you crazy? Off, Zuri!"

But on a hunch, Nina makes a phone call to Jose, who picks up an over-the-counter pregnancy test on his way home. The results are unequivocal—there will be a child.

Eight months later, Nina is on the bed again, and, suddenly, here is Zuri climbing aboard, all over her again, ignoring her protests, pushing and sniffing now at Nina's big belly, trying to cuddle. Within the hour, Nina's water breaks, and labor begins.

"Zuri feels a lot of things, and she expresses them," Nina says. "Sometimes you don't get them right away. She's very gentle to the baby. She's so gentle to me, she cuddles up when I don't feel well. She's very protective, too. She doesn't vocalize too much because she's trained not to, but she saved my life when we were abroad in Serbia and stray dogs attacked me. It was terrifying. I heard them all growling and coming at us. She fought right back. The howl that came out of my sweet girl—it was unearthly, like a wolf. I can hear it now."

Nina's son, Stefan, nearly a year old, has just awakened from his nap; his mother settles him with Zuri on the floor. He is a beautiful boy, with his mother's dark eyes and dark curly hair. He can toss Zuri's tennis ball about two inches before she pounces to retrieve it. And when they both tire, the baby lies comfortably against the capacious furry flanks.

A call to Fidelco's animal husbandry experts just before Stefan's birth yielded some advice on introducing this strange-smelling new interloper into the tight duo. "They told me to have Jose bring the receiving blanket and the little infant hat home from the hospital and give them to Zuri before he brought us home the next day. It had both our scents. I think she got the right message."

Parenthood has presented its challenges; when Stefan ran a fever, Jose had to leave work to come home and administer medicine, since Nina is unable to. But even Stefan has made his accommodations; as Nina hoists him into his high chair for a snack of yogurt, he bobs like a baby bird, following the spoon with open mouth. Their faces are nearly touching as she feeds him, and it works.

Comic relief arrives; Jose has returned from a trip to the gro-

Charlie and Robbie Kaman's shared love of and devotion to German shepherds led to a breeding operation that would eventually become the Fidelco Guide Dog Foundation. Since 1960, the couple's vision for Fidelco has promoted freedom and independence for people throughout North America by providing them with the highest-quality guide dogs.

The German shepherd is a model of intelligence, good temperament, and stability. Fidelco's German shepherds are bred from the strongest bloodlines to create a breed within a breed, worthy of the responsibility of guiding their human partners.

As a teenaged dog lover Dave Darr (shown here in the plaid shirt) fostered puppies for the Kamans. Seeing a guide dog in action turned him on to his true calling.

Kids and dogs—has there ever been a better combination? The Watch Me Grow program allows school classes to adopt a litter of puppies ready to enter the six-month guide dog training program, and follow their progress as they prepare to be teamed up with human partners.

Nina Bektic's path to her dog, Zuri, began many years ago in her native Sarajevo, where as a child she dealt with losing her sight during her country's civil war. She describes her match with Zuri as "very much a love story."

While they're with foster families, puppies attend puppy class at Fidelco several Saturdays a month for early training exercises. Puppy day is always one of the most joyful at Fidelco, as foster parents proudly watch their charges prepare for the responsibilities ahead.

Courtney Tabor's determination to walk across the stage to receive her high school diploma by herself—with a guide dog—brought her to Meeka. Since then they've made a great team through college and beyond.

Eddie Tabor communicates with his dog, Quinn, in ways he "can't explain to anyone else." The two young gentlemen have navigated the busy halls of Eddie's high school with freedom and confidence, and are now enjoying the challenges of college life together.

"I was always failing gym class and I didn't know why." As a child with undiagnosed vision problems, Vicky Nolan thought she was just naturally clumsy. Then her vision went completely. Today she's a competitive athlete who, with her first dog, Angus (shown here in the classroom where she teaches), and her successor dog, Vegas, has represented Canada in international competitions in Germany and at the 2008 Paralympics in Beijing.

Advocacy always came naturally to Janet LaBreck who, along with four of her siblings, lost her sight as a child to retinitis pigmentosa. Today she heads the Massachusetts Commission for the Blind, traveling far and wide and attending high-level governmen meetings with her dog, Osbourne, always at her side.

David Bearden, who's been a single parent almost as long as he has been blind, is not one to be sidelined by hardships. He fought to keep custody of his three infant children when an accident took his sight and his wife left him; he's traveled across the state of Florida as a disability activist and a crusader for the rights of service dogs; with his dog, Upton, he gets to carry out his love of singing on stage; and he is a dedicated foster and adoptive parent—as his recent award for Foster Parent of the Year can attest. *(Courtesy of David Bearden)*

Today David is a grandfather to Kadin and has been a foster parent to fifty-four boys and counting. He is also the adoptive father of one son and is currently in the process of adopting three young brothers. David considers Upton a full partner in his work with the children and an integral part of the growing Bearden family. *(Courtesy of David Bearden)*

Unique, a female shepherd, made headlines in July 2009 when lightning struck her eighty-three-year-old blind caretaker's house and caused a raging fire. Calmly and carefully, she led him out of the house to safety amid the chaos of the fire and a still-raging thunderstorm. Though not always so publicized, these noble dogs perform small miracles every day.

With each new foster family, volunteer, or litter of puppies, our Fidelco family is growing.

cery store. "The people at the store were glad to see me," he says. "Nina strikes fear in the hearts of people at ShopRite. If there's a sale, she'll be there and she will not be denied."

They married on New Year's Eve 2008; Stefan was born in February. Their budget is tight; they are saving to buy a condo. Nina is in a hurry for that, too. Jose says he is well aware that he is married to a very determined woman—and woe unto anyone who messes with his bride, from a produce manager who's failed to stock an advertised special to an intransigent bureaucrat at the huge Veterans Administration health facility in nearby Montrose where they both work.

Jose is on the maintenance staff and Nina is in communications, where she fields emergency calls, both medical and psychiatric, on the 180-acre facility that makes up the Montrose Campus of the Hudson Valley Health Care System. Jose offers an example of his wife's uncompromising sense of justice. "The transportation department was giving veterans with disabilities two to three minutes to get from one building to another to catch a bus. If you're wearing a prosthetic or in a wheelchair, you're not going to make it in three minutes. Nina called the head of transportation and said, 'What's going on there? These are our veterans and some of them can't run.'" Now the announcements are made fifteen minutes ahead of departure. And, says Jose, "No driver would ever dare give them less time because they would have to deal with . . . *her*."

It's not petulance, it's human rights, she insists. She and Jose have been refused apartments because of Zuri, or asked to post exorbitant damage deposits. Amazed, Jose has been educated on sighted folks' unthinking patronizing of the blind. When Jose accompanied Nina to an obstetrical appointment, the receptionist ignored her and spoke only to Jose until Nina quieted the bustling clinic with a loud declaration: "I'm not deaf or stupid and I'm the one having the appointment. If you want to know if I have an insurance card, ask me."

Delis and restaurants often turn them away. On Nina's first Mother's Day, when Jose took her and Stefan to a restaurant on Fordham Road in the Bronx for lunch, management would not let Zuri in, though service dogs are permitted by law. They have a pending lawsuit. She just can't let it go.

"Since I lost my sight, my goals in life have changed. So has the way I look at things. I think I've matured within my disability, from the point in which I was just trying to be avoiding society to where I'm actually confronting society when it comes to discrimination. It's a big change. Sometimes it is frustrating, but it's all worth it in the end. It just makes you stronger."

In the spring of 2008, she and Zuri went to Washington, D.C., as representatives from the Association for Vision Rehabilitation and Employment, the agency that placed Nina in her position at the VA. "We went to discuss and lobby for the modernization of the JWOD Act, as well as other disability-related laws." JWOD—Javits-Wagner-O'Day—provides job training and opportunities for the disabled. It was created in 1938 during FDR's administration as the Wagner-O'Day Program, allowing the disabled to make and sell mops and brooms to the government. In 1971, Senator Jacob Javits helped update its programs.

Nina, who uses sophisticated adaptive equipment to do her job, says the program is sorely in need of revamping to fit the times. "The mission in Washington was to meet with congressmen and senators and to speak to media, to make sure that the modernization of the law does occur. Things change. And research suggests that because of the baby boomers, the population of legally blind people is probably going to increase very significantly."

All went well except for an altercation Zuri had with another guide dog. Since she and Nina were attacked by the stray dogs in Serbia, Zuri has had problems with other dogs. "It's not offensive," Nina says. "It's an overly protective defensive mode. She thinks anything closer than ten feet is too close." She and Fidelco trainers worked to overcome the issue before the trip, but it remains a worry. "I know it in my heart—that moment in Serbia was the cause of Zuri's post-traumatic stress."

Post-traumatic stress syndrome is well understood in this home. Jose sees its effects in the VA hospital wards and at the support groups he still attends as an Army veteran. Nina knows the potentially destructive force of her own memories. And she says it was Zuri, absolutely Zuri, who helped her walk away from them and into the light. "There is no other way I would have found my happiness. She led me out. Zuri's like my logo, my sign of independence."

Their home has another strong talisman. Dimitri is here, in safe repose on a shelf next to Nina's Bible. The beloved old toy is off-limits to Stefan, who is allowed to give him an occasional kiss. The child will be raised with what Nina hopes is a natural sensitivity to the needs—and the potential—of the disabled. She wishes she had been more aware herself as a child. She is not proud to recall her own understanding of blindness before it befell her.

The memory goes back to Belgrade. It had rained overnight and the streets were wet and slick as a blind man made his way haltingly. He blundered into a hole filled with water and mud and behind him, a group of schoolgirls giggled. Nina was among them.

"It was funny then," she recalls. "I was young, into sports, playing tennis. Human rights was not something I was focused on. But looking back at it, I'd call up the agency responsible for the street and have them fix the problem."

"And heaven help them," says Jose, "if they didn't get it done fast enough."

CHAPTER THREE

COURTNEY AND EDDIE

*It made Mom a little sad the first day I got Meeka. I had
always held on to her arm.*

—Courtney Tabor

*The new baby is Tim and Marie Tabor's first child, a
beautiful, dark-haired girl, born in June 1987. All had
been well on her first postnatal checkup at two weeks. But at
her one-month exam, the pediatrician was concerned that
Courtney's eyes did not appear to focus at all.*

*Marie can see it herself now; the baby should be attentive
to a bright object, a sudden movement above her head, but
she shows no reaction. And here in the consulting ophthalmologist's office, she and Tim wait nervously as the doctor
puts drops in Courtney's eyes and bends down to examine
her. At last he straightens and tells them flatly, as though
he might be discussing a milk allergy, "Courtney is blind.
And she will be blind for life."*

Marie is just twenty-five, still sleep-deprived and bouncing between postpartum joys and jitters. And now she is shocked speechless. Her mouth is open, but she can form no words. How can the doctor say such a thing—and so bluntly, so matter-of-factly? Finally, as she reaches for the baby, Marie is able to croak—barely, crazily, "Thank you."

She and Tim leave the office and head for the parking lot, still unable to speak. He goes numbly to work. Heading home with Courtney, she runs into a friend who begins to coo at the newborn, and Marie can finally force a sound.

"I started crying," she recalls, "and I couldn't stop."

Shortly after, the Tabors drove to Hartford from their home in Andover, Connecticut, and got a full and final diagnosis from a pediatric group specializing in vision problems. Leber's congenital amaurosis is a rare inherited eye disease that is usually diagnosed within the first few months of life. It causes impaired development of the retina, and interferes with visual messages being sent to the brain; whatever minimal sight exists may soon be lost. Courtney could detect only light and dark with her left eye. For a time, she had some sight in her right eye, augmented with glasses when she was very small. Though there has been some promising experimentation with gene therapy, there is currently no treatment or cure.

Nor were there any signposts for a panicky new mother to follow twenty-two years ago. Marie lay awake with hundreds of questions—and few answers: "What could I do for a sightless baby? How could I keep her from hurting herself when she was learning to walk? How would she go to school, dress herself, have friends? I realized it was up to me to figure it out."

So Marie found her voice—a different, bolder voice, she realizes now—and she began to make calls. So very many calls. She found a local support group for parents of visually impaired children, and researched her baby's condition. They took Courtney to Children's Hospital Boston, where she was enrolled in a study of children with Leber's. In the course of her research, Marie learned that the odds were one in four of having a second child born with the disease, but of all the families she met with Leber's-affected sons or daughters, none had been dealt that double misfortune.

The Tabors felt that Courtney would surely benefit from having a sibling. And when her brother, Eddie, was born in October 1991, says Marie, "I looked at him, I watched his eyes, and I knew right away. There was no question in my mind." When Eddie's Leber's diagnosis was confirmed soon after, she recalls, "there were just five other couples in the United States who had two children with Leber's."

Both Courtney and Eddie were born with 20/200 vision, which categorizes them as legally blind. "Back then, it seemed to me that they had a tremendous amount of vision," says Marie, "even though they didn't. As they got older, it got progressively worse." And so they became a very tight threesome—together everywhere, all the time. Until they got their guide dogs, Courtney and Eddie were, she says, "attached at my arms and hips, twenty-four/seven, since birth."

Now divorced from Tim and using her maiden name, Russo, Marie is recalling those early years in her office at North Branford High School in central Connecticut. She works here as Eddie's school aide and Braille translator. The shelves are stacked with audiobook discs and thick white Braille textbooks, which can run to fifty volumes each. Outside in the corridor, high-decibel cheerleaders are mustering for a bus ride to a rival school, and two boys' sports teams are adding to the din. Eddie is just a minute's walk away from his mother this afternoon, as he has been most of his life. Right now he is convening the after-school chess club he started, in the company of his Fidelco guide dog, Quinn.

Marie taught herself Braille when Courtney was learning to read it in elementary school. Since Braille-ing of class materials was done by a visiting vision specialist, there was often a delay that would put Courtney chronically behind her classmates—unless Marie could provide the translations faster. She broadened her skills by taking online instruction from the Library of Congress. Once Courtney showed an aptitude for studying languages, Marie tapped out lessons and homework in French, Italian, and Spanish "with all the accents. And math—I can do all levels of math."

Courtney and Eddie were accompanied by aides throughout elementary and middle school, and had cane mobility instruction to help them get around. Once Courtney entered high school, Marie became her aide and Braille translator, salaried by the school system; when they moved to North Branfield and Eddie reached high school, she provided the same services there. For a time, Marie also did Braille-ing for a first grader in the district.

And so the years have passed, in countless pages of raised-dot symbols for trig functions and quadratic equations, for elements on the periodic table, for study outlines dating the Monroe Doctrine, women's suffrage, and Renaissance art. Marie types the characters into a computer with translating software. A Braille printer in the corner clicks out page after page.

With Eddie about to graduate from high school and Courtney on the cusp of finishing college with her guide dog, Meeka, Marie's two-decade-long marathon is nearly run. She will be remarrying and relocating to Massachusetts a month after

Eddie's graduation. She is not sure how they all would have gotten to this sunny, wide-open place in their lives without the two dogs around to walk her babies out into the wider world.

"The dogs are the best thing that could have happened to both my kids. Before, they were always very much around me, not nearly as independent as they are now. I think the dogs have helped them to be a little bit more outgoing. And they feel better. You just have to be happy with dogs like these. You step away and come back and the dog loves you, it's so glad to see you. They're just fun."

And they are hardworking animals, though Meeka may occasionally moan like a balky teenager when it's time to get up for an early class. Marie admits the two shepherds faced their toughest challenge in conquering a mother's instinctive doubts: "To trust those dogs with my children's lives is the most incredible thing. And I do now, absolutely. But it was a long, long way to get there."

Marie is a smiling, easygoing woman with a fairly wicked sense of humor. What else can you do but laugh when your blind daughter blunders into the Christmas tree and knocks it over? How else can you cope with the dissonant and constant babble of strangers in your home, mellifluous audiobook narrators engaging in a lively *contrappunto* with the oblique, robotic voices of adaptive software reading e-mail and documents aloud? "Our normal," Marie says, "is anything but." Thus she and her children are lovingly merciless with one another, reliant on a dry, intimate sarcasm to defuse life's more absurd moments. Here's Eddie's tender way to summon his older sister:

"Hey! Blindette!"

Despite the good humor, there is an edge to Marie's voice as she describes the uphill journey to this point, and the isolation they have all felt at times. "My whole life changed when Court-ney was born—and not because I was a mother. Suddenly I've got this blind kid, in a world that's not as friendly to her as you'd hope. You become even more protective and—when you have to—more aggressive. I used to get so angry at people in the store because they're so rude. People are just so rude."

Throughout her children's lives, affronts have been constant and unavoidable—yet somehow, always surprising. A mundane trip to the supermarket turned sharply painful when a bagger peered down at Courtney and snapped at her, "Are you day-dreaming or are you cross-eyed?"

Marie says there was a lot of the "mama bear syndrome" oper-ative when it came to protecting and defending the children; she confesses that taking on that role required a bit of a personal-ity change. "I was a very meek kind of person," she says. "If I hadn't made myself become as aggressive and outspoken, I don't think my kids would be where they are today. I had to fight for everything that they have in terms of their education and their rights."

She describes the relentless, humbling rhythms familiar to many parents of disabled children: Call about a needed service. Call back. Call three, four times more and get the name of a supervisor. Call her three times, four, never stop, don't dare let it rest. Sit on a doorstep if you have to, sweet-talk a secretary. Call again. It was exhausting and frustrating, but the alternative was unthinkable: "I had to get into people's faces—and I didn't have a problem doing it. I wanted my kids to be successful. I didn't want them lumped into an awful statistic I'd heard—that 80 percent of the blind population isn't employed. I was think-ing, 'There's no way that's going to happen to my kids.'"

It has been a solitary struggle. She says that her ex-husband, whom she divorced when Courtney was in high school and Eddie in seventh grade, "was not the type to go to meetings." And many of her own peers lacked the comfort level or the tenacity to stay in close touch. "I lost a lot of friends because my life was so different. You're trying to find things for your kid to get involved in and yet all your friends are off doing soccer and basketball and all that visual stuff. You don't have that connection with the rest of the people in town."

She and the children were such an inseparable trio, she says, because "I didn't have babysitting help, not even with my family, my parents. Nobody knew how to talk to them. Just because they're blind, people seem to think that they're mentally challenged. The injustice and absurdity of those attitudes still totally blows me away."

Socializing a blind child, she says, is the most frequent topic in the many workshops she's attended for parents of visually impaired children. "Everybody has that issue—where their kids don't have that normal social life. Honestly, you do everything you can to get them involved, but it's so hard because you're expecting other kids to come forward. Your kids can't just get up and walk over to a group on a playground or ride a bike to a friend's house. So there isn't a whole lot of social life unless you get them involved in stuff. And believe me, I tried to get them involved in everything known to man."

She says she worked just as hard to avoid any semblance of pity or overindulgence that would leave them vulnerable and unprepared. Courtney and Eddie had chores—and consequences if they were left undone. They learned to take showers alone and dress themselves and pick up their rooms. They went to regular school at the same ages as their peers, albeit in the company of their school aides and Marie, who was a regular presence in their classrooms.

Like many little girls, Courtney started asking for a dog of her own at age six. But she did not want the standard cuddly puppy. She had met a blind woman with a guide dog who let her pet the animal and hold its harness. She told the child about the amazing things the dog was able to do to help her get around. From the beginning, Courtney hated her cane. And meeting that first guide dog, she formed a judgment that she still voices today: "The cane always seemed so unfriendly. A dog is so much happier than a stick."

When Marie explained that she had to be much older to care for a dog of her own, Courtney said that was fine—she would wait. But she always spoke of it as a given; the minute she was old enough, she intended to walk through the rest of her life with a guide dog. "She was such a good kid and wanted it so much," says Marie. "How could I possibly say no?"

Courtney was always a good and eager student. But homework can take an average of two to three times longer than the hours that sighted students must put in on the same assignments. There is no highlighting or skimming to review material for a test. As she grew, so did the array and quality of adaptive equipment available. By high school, Courtney's large, unwieldy Braille keyboard had been replaced by a compact $6,000 Braille-Note computer that helped her go online, read books, and prepare her homework papers. Her school pushed to get the purchase approved for a student exceptional by any standards. Brian Morin, then the district's director of special education, explained the acquisition to a reporter for the *Hartford Courant*:

"We went aggressively because of Courtney's ability. We knew she would soar."

And every semester's honor roll did carry her name—despite a sudden shock in the summer between her junior and senior years. The pressure within Courtney's right eye increased to twice its normal level, radiating a sharp, searing pain. In an effort to relieve the pressure, a laser surgeon cut a series of tiny slits in the iris. But it was unsuccessful. Courtney's only recourse to stop the pain was to have the entire lens removed, and with it, what was left of her sight. Without a lens to focus images, only a sense of light and dark remains, and that may disappear some-day as well.

Then, as now, Courtney refused to dwell on that possibil-ity. She told the same *Courant* reporter, "I can't look at it as a big deal or I'd be a depressed person." Instead, she focused on the dog. That same summer, she worked on her application. Fidelco was and is the only guide dog school in New England. And the Tabors had already encountered some of their dogs.

"We knew of a teacher in Courtney's school that fostered Fidelco puppies and would bring them in to class," says Marie. "We started doing fund-raisers with them in the school. One thing led to another." She had looked into other guide dog orga-nizations with residential training that required a stay of three to four weeks in other states, with minimal visits from family. Marie was having none of that. "I was not going to let my kids leave me for that long, no way. I thought it was much better for them to come here."

When Courtney's application came in, there was some appre-hension at Fidelco. The unwritten age requirement for getting a dog had long been eighteen; Courtney knew that she was applying early at seventeen, with a year of high school to finish. And Fidelco training staff and administrators had a few misgivings about guide dogs in secondary school.

Quite simply, there are too many unpredictable variables. Their shepherds could end up as unwitting—and distracted—mascots. Students have been known to tempt them with everything from peanut butter to pizza crusts. Crowds are the toughest kind of work for guide dogs, and the hallways could be too clamorous. Above all, teenagers weren't as prepared for the full responsibility of a dog that, for bonding purposes, had to be cared for by their handler alone.

Yet there was something very sensible, directed, and purposeful about this girl. She voiced a strong desire for more independence—something the placement staff always liked to hear in a potential client. She clearly had plans for herself. And Courtney had a very specific goal in getting a guide dog a bit earlier than most when she initially spoke with then-director George Salpietro. She told him in their first phone conversation that she wanted to walk across the stage to get her high school diploma by herself—with a guide dog.

Warning Courtney that he had strong doubts that they could get her a dog so early, George agreed to at least visit her at RHAM High School (a regional school district acronym for the towns of Hebron, Andover, and Marlborough) in the company of his own guide dog, Oskar.

"We had a ball together that day," George recalls. "And I was even more impressed by her determination." He noted that Courtney's cane skills were good—a requirement for all applicants. The students seemed friendly and cooperative. And as they walked along, Courtney kept up her full-court press: It would be so incredible to graduate with a guide dog, to have it before she left for college and had to navigate in a strange environment. Really, it made perfect sense—right?

Finally, midway through her senior year, Courtney got the call. There was a dog well suited to her that had just finished its training. And they just might pull off that commencement if she and the dog worked effectively together.

In the month and a half before he placed Meeka with Courtney, Dave Darr set about fine-tuning the dog's skills by taking her to his daughter Hailey's high school in Winsted, Connecticut. He remembers: "Meeka was fine in the hallway—animated enough to make the changes that a long day at high school requires. She could roll from class to class, she could sit quietly for a full class period. She was alert and ready, yet not so animated that she seemed like any teenager—*I want to get out of here and go go go*. It was a nice middle ground."

He took her to the school a few times, and Meeka grew more acclimated and proficient during each visit. This was a very people-friendly dog that could also maintain some poise on the job; navigating the loud, bumptious corridors and staying on task was no small accomplishment. "The way teenagers handle themselves through a hallway," says Dave, "is *not* normal."

When he felt the dog was ready, they decided to start her training with Courtney during her school's April break. He brought Meeka to the Tabors' condo in Andover, having already warned Courtney that her new companion might totally ignore her at first. "We tell everyone not to expect the big moment where everything moves in slow motion, the door opens up, and the dog goes leaping into the arms of her new handler," Dave says. "That never happens. Ever."

Except with Meeka, who bounded straight to Courtney and engaged in a high-excitement lovefest, dog and girl both rolling on the floor. Dave watched them open-mouthed. "Never before and never since have I seen anything like it," he says. "And no, I cannot explain it."

Though she had long wanted the dog for Courtney, Marie was surprised by her own reaction. "The day Dave brought the dog and Courtney walked out of the house with her, it just freaked me out," she says. "I cried. It was difficult to see her go off, even knowing the dog will keep her safe. I was still thinking, It's just a dog. Just a dog."

And this sharp-eyed, affable animal striding off with her daughter was off-limits to Marie and Eddie. Steering clear of a new dog was hard on a little brother who had never had a pet. And it felt unnatural for Marie to stand by and watch the struggles that ensued. Meeka was upsetting the dynamics of their tight little household. "The first few months, they don't want the dog interacting with anybody else in the house but its handler. That was stressful. I'm telling Courtney, 'You've got to get up earlier, get yourself ready, and then take care of the baby.' Getting organized was hard. It took a lot of practice."

Even without worrying about getting to school that first week, it was a daily ordeal for a teenage girl to get herself and the dog up, take Meeka out, feed her, bolt breakfast, and dress and harness the dog by the time Dave got to the door at 8:30. Outdoors, there was some anxiety and impatience as Courtney gave Meeka the signal to relieve herself ("get busy!") so she could locate and bag the dog's waste, as Dave had taught her, and get on with her own morning toilette.

"She wasn't timing things right because of the dog," Marie recalls. "The dog senses stress. So when Courtney gets stressed, Meeka gets stressed." It was Dave's delicate task to ease all three anxious females down the road. "He spent three weeks with us,"

Marie says. "He practically lived at my house, from sunup to sundown. Five, six, seven days a week sometimes. He brought his kids, his dog. It was great. They get involved in your life. And with our crazy household, it took the patience of a saint."

June 22, graduation day for the class of 2005 at RHAM High School. Courtney's new extended family is in the front row: Marie and Eddie, George and Marie Salpietro—and George's dog Oskar, wearing a black tie. And Dave Darr. And the Fidelco trainer Ron Labonte and his wife, Cindy.

Courtney and Meeka make their way to the stage so she can deliver her valedictory speech. All week, local TV news and print reporters have been trumpeting this achievement, dubbing her the "blind valedictorian." That, and some of their other well-meant but unfortunate phraseology, had not pleased her.

"Courtney has suffered from blindness all her life. . . . "

No, she has not suffered, she told one reporter, this is just the life God gave her, which is pretty fine at the moment. And she wished it were understood: the honor of being chosen valedictorian was hardly a sympathy vote. She has the bona fides—the honors and Advanced Placement courses, the activities, election to the National Honor Society, the solid-platinum GPA. She is a mainstay of the chorus, can sing "Ave Maria" in four languages. . . .

As she places her Braille text on the podium, three TV news cameras focus on the pretty, poised young woman and the dog sitting patiently alongside, wearing her harness— and her own shepherd-sized cap and gown. The speech goes well, the applause is thunderous, and the walk back to her seat is blessedly unremarkable.

When, finally, the dreamed-of moment arrives, Court-
ney and Meeka walk back onto the stage; the graduate
reaches for her diploma, and it is probably a good thing that
she cannot see the adults in the Fidelco family row. They
are a sorry, soggy sight, dabbing at their eyes and passing
tissues.

Dave has been watching Marie, who is radiant, almost
levitating out of her chair. He has spent weeks marvel-
ing at her daily devotions to these children. And he has sat
with Marie for hours, joking to relieve the tension, and
reassuring her, over and over: "I trained Meeka myself,
tailor-made her for Courtney. I give you my word: they're
going to be fine."

Marie's eye is on the diploma, clutched tightly against
Courtney's gown, and Dave is thinking, "That's Marie's,
too. She's earned this moment."

Over the summer, the fraught mornings mellowed into routine; Meeka and Courtney became a tighter, more functional
team. And Marie began to notice subtle changes in how her
daughter advanced to meet the world. "Courtney is very shy, but
if you get her engaged, she can be very social. Meeka is a social
butterfly. I think she has brought Courtney out of her shell. She's
just a fun, loving dog. I think they matched them really well. I
don't know how they do it."

Courtney's stellar academic record got her into her heart's
desire: Middlebury College, in Vermont. She passed on an Ivy
League school whose admissions officer admitted they hadn't
had a blind student in over twenty years. "I didn't want to be
their guinea pig," Courtney told her mother. Dave Darr offered
some advice on navigating the harsh northern winters, which

could be hard on a guide dog: Courtney should be wary of frost-bitten ears, sore paws, and navigational confusion once paths and curbs were buried in snow and ice. And of course, should she have any problems with Meeka, a trainer would come to the campus and help them work it out.

In August, a week before the rest of the incoming freshman class, Marie, Courtney, and Meeka drove north, to settle her in and begin orientation on the winding, hilly paths crisscrossing the campus. Courtney was assigned a double room as a single; getting acclimated with Meeka would be more focused without a roommate. Clothes were stowed, the bed made, Meeka's food dish and bedding arranged. It was time.

Marie says that except for that shocking diagnosis so long ago, the looming separation was the most excruciating moment she faced as a parent. A team of kind professionals from the college's office for disabilities was on hand to help Courtney and Meeka settle in, but Marie was not ready to surrender her firstborn.

"When it came time to leave her, I just couldn't face it. I was bawling. They grabbed me because I couldn't let go of Courtney. And of course she's crying and scared. She didn't know anybody. They pulled me away and turned me around. And without me even knowing, they put her in a car. I turned around and she was gone."

The shock of separation hit like a thunderbolt; Marie's knees buckled and she fell to the ground. "I just went down like a tree. But they had to do that—they had to get her away and down to business. I drove home alone, and I was a mess. I stopped many times. I cried all the way, called my sister. It was really hard."

Even after the sting of that parting subsided, some of the phone calls were heartrending. Especially early one December morning after a heavy night's snow.

"Mom. Mom, are you there?"

The voice is small and very scared beneath the cell phone crackle. Courtney is disoriented, lost, and panicky. She just wasn't thinking when she harnessed Meeka and started off to check her mail very early this morning—way too early. The pathways weren't cleared yet after this, Courtney's first major Vermont snowfall. Her commands are useless; Meeka can't find left or right, or any semblance of a path. They have blundered for forty-five minutes in the frigid, maddening silence; she can hear only the dog's panting and the wind.

"It's so cold out here. There's no one else around. Mom, I don't know what to do."

Mom is a four-hour drive away, and she is frantic, but she tries to push the panic from her voice with some gruff common sense.

"Why are you calling me? Call public safety, they'll come get you. . . . "

"I can't do this, I just can't. What was I thinking?"

And Marie hears another, more distant voice in the background. It's a passerby, offering help.

"Mom? Mom. It's okay now, he's leading us home."

"My mother is my hero," says Courtney. "She is just incredible. She's always been behind Eddie and me, one hundred and fifty percent. She fought for everything we needed and she taught me how to do it."

Weeks from finishing their undergraduate career, Courtney and Meeka are relaxing in the airy common room of the spacious dorm suite she shares with three roommates. Meeka is surely among the most outgoing of Fidelco shepherds, bounding over for a hello, laying her big head on a knee, nosing a shoulder until a word from Courtney sends her to lie quietly—for a bit. After four years on this postcard-perfect campus, despite snows, library all-nighters, parties, and ever-changing class schedules, Courtney says that Meeka has proved adaptable and steadfast.

"It doesn't take her long to learn a new route, let's say a class in a different room or building. She learns them really, really fast—two days, tops. I find that we work together a lot better now than we did a couple of years ago. A lot of it has to do with the fact that she's sensing how confident I am." Even after all this time together, she finds herself surprised at the dog's deep and unerring memory. "I live in a different dorm every year. At one point in my sophomore year, I went back to my freshman dorm to visit someone. She brought me right back to my old room. She remembers."

Things were not so smooth at first. A Fidelco instructor was dispatched within a month of her arrival at Middlebury to assess the problems. "This campus is kind of difficult to learn," Courtney says. "It's not laid out in block pattern." She was having difficulty getting oriented, and her stress was affecting the dog as well.

First, the Fidelco instructor observed them; then they worked to correct the problems. Courtney was given a Gentle Leader collar for Meeka that encourages a dog to keep its head up, stop sniffing things on the ground, and stay focused. "It's taken a few years to learn how to deal with different things as they come up," Courtney says. "The Fidelco instructors came and helped me a few times—that's one of the best things about them. I just need to call and they're like, 'All right, where are you and when do you want us? We'll come, stay in a hotel, and work things out.'"

And unless you count that snowstorm incident—Courtney

can't *believe* that her mother is still telling that story—Meeka's navigational skills are now better than she could have imagined: "She's so smooth. People point out that she's just brought me around something, a hole or an object, and I don't even realize it. It happened recently. Someone said, 'Oh, don't you know what was in the sidewalk?' It was a broken bottle or something. She brought me right around it and I didn't even know there was a hazard."

Meeka's energy level is a clear sign she carries the tenacious DNA of those Bavarian shepherds that have bolstered the Fidelco line. "She's not the type of dog that always wants to be out of harness," Courtney says. "She works any time of day. I've awakened her at three in the morning to go print out a paper and she comes right along. She's got a lot of energy. She's a college kid."

As such, she's been a big dog on campus. Theirs is a familiar profile striding along the paths toward their hilltop dorm. "Having a dog made it ten times better socially than it would have been without her," Courtney says. "Meeka was an icebreaker in many ways. People love to see a dog on campus. I had a girl come up to me crying once, saying, 'I miss my dog.'"

Just how the sighted world perceives her has been a sensitive issue since she was a child, Courtney admits. And a large part of her new comfort level is related to how Meeka defines her in a public space. "Having the dog cues people that I'm blind. And people aren't really as afraid. Before I got the dog, I remember walking with my cane in the mall with my mom, and a kid said, 'Mama, what's that?' The mom pulled the kid away and said, 'We don't have to talk about that.'"

Training in Hartford with Dave Darr and Meeka, she overheard another conversation as they walked along a busy street.

"A little girl asked her dad, 'What's the doggie doing?' And he said, 'Oh, he's helping that lady, she can't see.' It felt better."

Academics have never been a problem, even at this rigorous institution. And keeping up with assignments, friends, and the world has gotten easier with the digital equipment here in her dorm room. "I have JAWS, the adaptive software, on my laptop, I have a Braille computer—it's very cool. And now I have a color-identifying kit that helps you dress. My mom gave it to me." She has but to place a sock or shirt by the machine's spectrographic sensor and a prim British voice intones, "Very dark blue."

Meeka is a bit restless, pushing a tennis ball forward with her nose, pacing through the kitchen and the hall entrance where her harness hangs above a collegiate welter of scarves, sneakers, and Ugg boots. She settles back down at Courtney's feet with a resigned sigh.

"I can't imagine going back to life without a dog," Courtney says. "I think she has opened up a lot for me in terms of independence. She's given me a lot more confidence in my own capability. The trust is a cool thing, too. Being able to put my trust in her is really special. But having her also trust me feels good, too. I love the bond, and it's a different bond than anyone has with their pet. Not to minimize the pet relationship—but this is unlike anything else. She got a little stomach-sick the other day and I was just all over it, watching her every second, like I'm her mother. That's a very special bond."

When Courtney brought a boyfriend into their relationship early in her freshman year, that bond was not threatened; more problematic was Meeka's inclination to share the love. While she wouldn't go so far as to call Meeka a guy magnet, Courtney does consider her a Cupid of sorts. "My fiancé tells me all the time, 'I would not have come and talked to you if you didn't have a dog.' I'm like, 'Hey, why not?' And he said, 'I'd be too scared.'"

Chris Abbott, then a sophomore premed student from Maine, had never seen a working guide dog before Courtney and Meeka walked into the campus arts center for the semester's first meeting of returning chamber singers and freshmen hoping to join. "I looked at the dog and at Courtney," Chris recalls. "Let's say I was interested all the way around." He struck up a conversation about Meeka, and they walked together to the traditional first-rehearsal dinner at Proctor Hall. Later that week, the three of them took a late-night stroll all over campus. The following Monday, "after a little research on the Internet," Chris used a pin and an index card to punch out a little note in Braille, asking Courtney out.

Dating with a dog has been an adventure, he concedes, especially when Meeka became so smitten with Courtney's suitor that a Fidelco trainer had to drive up and stage an intervention of sorts. "Meeka's in love with my fiancé," Courtney explains. "She became attached to him very, very quickly. Probably the biggest problem I've had is trying to figure out how to make her pay attention when he's around."

Tommy Mourad, a Fidelco instructor who worked with them at Chris's family home in Maine when Courtney spent the summer there, had this advice: You can't really keep Chris away from the dog. But you can make it so that when she's working, he cannot have any interaction. He can't talk to her in a goofy, high-pitched "let's play" voice, or make eye contact with her when she is in harness.

After all three of them worked with the instructor, Courtney is able to give an effective correction if Meeka pays too much attention to their mutual beloved. "It's all about establishing the right time and place for her behavior," she says.

Now that those ground rules have been established and reasonably enforced, Meeka is nearly always with them, save for a trip to the Florida theme parks when the dog stayed with Marie. If they run into any more difficulties, they will call in the experts again and fix it. Both will tell you: the strongest love is adaptive. It has to be, when you have never actually seen your true love's face. Unlike many Fidelco clients whose vision loss came later in life, Courtney says she does not feel so acutely the lack of something she never really had. "My visual memory is pretty poor. I did have some color sense when I was younger. But it was a pretty rapid decline."

Blindness will never come between them, Chris is sure, as long as they give the disability its space. "It's not just, 'Okay, she's blind, no big deal,'" he says. "You have to be constantly aware of it. You have to talk—about all aspects of it. Open communications are important. And you have to train yourself. Don't leave a cabinet door open, put your shoes where she won't trip over them. And, of course, never pet the dog when she's working."

He and Meeka are boon companions when she is off duty now, playing ball and just hanging out. Chris can take the dog out to relieve herself, but he does not feed her or give her treats. "Courtney's got to be the mom," he says. Courtney has also made some adaptive changes to help the relationship. Since she is never without her BrailleNote computer, she uses headphones with it more often. Says Chris, "The voice of the JAWS software can get a bit monotonous."

He says that his family in Belfast, Maine, has embraced their future daughter-in-law and her dog, without reservation. Their reaction, when he first invited Courtney and Meeka to his parents' vacation time-share in New Hampshire, was simply "What can we do to make her more comfortable here?" The Abbotts got their initial glimpse into the complex world of the disabled when they checked with the time-share management about having a dog visit despite their no-pets rule.

"Apparently, another family had tried passing their poodle off as a guide dog," says Chris. "But my dad convinced them Meeka was legitimate, and we all had a great time." Likewise, he has felt perfectly at ease in Marie's home—even on that raucous Thanksgiving in 2008 when Eddie had just gotten Quinn and the two dogs chased one another madly, gladly, around the dinner table. Their life together is simply the new normal: happy, comfortable—and, thanks to Meeka, bristling with small, unexpected, and amazing graces.

As is the tradition, Christmas Eve service at Belfast United Methodist Church is concluding with a tight, candlelit circle of worshippers in the sanctuary. At a nod from his father, who is the pastor here, Chris plunks a piano note to cue Courtney, who begins a solo rendition of "O Holy Night."

The notes soar, lovely and clear. All eyes are on the pastor's future daughter-in-law. But what's that sound?

A low whine. A canine rumble beneath the sweet soprano. The congregation begins to smile and titter as the disturbance grows louder and more insistent.

"Fall on your knees!

"O hear the angels' voices. . . . "

Awroooo.

Meeka is singing along with her partner—loudly,

unabashedly now. And the congregation is laughing at—
and loving—this four-legged blessing in its midst.

"She was very cute," says Chris. "But that was the last time we took Meeka to a concert." He expects that Courtney will pull him back into choral singing once they are both settled in graduate school in Maine. Having graduated in February 2008 from Middlebury, Chris spent the ensuing year working as an emergency medical technician for AmeriCorps in Searsport, Maine. Resettling in Maine after Courtney's graduation from Middlebury—magna cum laude—they will both be students again, Chris in medical school at the University of New England, and Courtney in graduate school at the University of Maine.

"I'm going to school for social work," she says. "I can see working in a school or a children's hospital. I think ultimately I'd like to do some sort of nonprofit work counseling families who have children with disabilities. There are plenty of people coping with disabilities who haven't yet traveled as far as I have. I'm pretty fortunate to have the help from my family that I don't think a lot of people have."

Neither sees limits on their future together. "Courtney can't wait to be a mom," Chris says. Someday, after medical school, and after his rigorous three-year residency, he would like to build his bride a house that will make her life easier—and cut down on the bruises. "It will have an open layout," he says, "with talking thermostats, a stove with a protective top for the burners . . . everything she needs."

They have not set a wedding date, but there is a lovely, delicate engagement ring on Courtney's finger, with three diamonds at its center. Chris says his choice was a practical one: "She uses her hands a lot, with the leash and harness, and I felt a solitaire setting was more likely to snag on things." This is true, but when he gave Courtney the ring on Christmas 2008, he also told her that the three brilliant stones are an apt symbol for their future together: "One for me, one for you—and one for Meeka."

Dave Darr remembers that for a kid with 20/200 vision, Eddie Tabor had pretty deadly aim with a water pistol. Five years ago, while he was instructing Courtney and Meeka, the big blond guy was a favorite target. Eddie has more vision than his sister— enough to describe the rudiments of a TV show or movie to her if the light in the room is right. And he clearly relished the role he had carved for himself as family trickster. At thirteen, Eddie put rubber spiders under his sister's pillow, closed doors so that she would blunder into them, and spookily enlarged her face on his Clarity Deskmate, a video magnifier with a fifteen-inch screen. In short, he was the model of a loving little brother.

And here is Eddie now at seventeen, smiling in the doorway of his mother's office with Quinn, a slender, coal black shepherd uncannily matched to his own thin, dark-haired good looks. As they settle in on the floor for a talk, the dog curls itself against Eddie, who absently strokes a paw between both hands. "He's such a great guy. I just love him," he says. "He is so right for me." Quinn returns the affection; though he weighs nearly eighty-five pounds, he has now managed to curl up in Eddie's lap.

Marie recalls phoning Dave Darr to tell him that Eddie would be applying for a dog somewhat early, as his sister had done. "We've been expecting your call," he told her. "I have a dog in mind." Marie wondered how that could possibly be, since he hadn't seen Eddie in four years.

"Yeah, but I remember Eddie."

After observing Eddie's first few months with Quinn, who is about to turn two, Marie says, "Once again they did it right, in terms of a match. Eddie is funny but very reserved, very calm. Dave had said, 'I have this dog, he's quite the gentleman. You'll see.' Eddie's very much a gentleman. But he's got that whole fun-loving side. And the dog has that, too. He likes to play tricks, just like Eddie. They're two peas in a pod. And I wonder: how do they do it? They're perfect together."

The two gentlemen are in discreet conference on the floor of Marie's office; Eddie says that Quinn will need a trip outside soon—yet no signal between them was detectable to an outsider. "I just know," Eddie says. "We communicate in ways I can't explain to anyone else."

He cannot believe he was ever iffy about getting a dog. Like his sister, he is not fond of his cane, and loathed the mobility lessons with it he has endured over the years. Nonetheless, he says he had a spell where he was not yet ready to give full control of his movement to a dog. "I think for a while I was just feeling that I wanted to use what vision I had. I didn't want to have to depend on something. Then I decided it would be better. I knew I would like the companionship. He's not just a cane, he's a living, breathing being. He's always there."

Marie believes that the visual impairment made it more difficult for her boy to navigate a social life—at least before the dog. With Courtney, she found, other girls seemed more nurturing and inclined to look out for her, lead her to a cafeteria line, describe food, and help her navigate. "It's definitely a lot different for my son because guys don't know how to do that, to be with somebody that's disabled," Marie says. "It's even worse when they get older. Eddie said a couple of weeks ago, 'I don't understand why I don't have more friends who are not blind or have a learning disability.' I said, 'I'm sorry—you're going to have to wait until college. Kids aren't grown up until then. Hopefully you'll find your niche a bit later, in the wider world.'"

Eddie is sure that seeing his sister's success with Meeka and watching the training process from such an intimate vantage point helped things go smoothly when Becky Cook, his Fidelco instructor, brought Quinn to him just before Thanksgiving 2008. Sure, he was nervous. But he says that Becky made the process "very cool and relaxed. We got the work done, but we joked a lot. And these people understand my issues without my having to explain it. It's such a relief to work with somebody who just gets it. Like, it's no big deal, it's just my life."

Classes have already started when Eddie walks into his high school lobby—without his cane. He is part of a new trio now: himself, Becky Cook, and the mighty Quinn. It's an intense togetherness, sunup to past sundown, and he is glad for a bit of downtime as Becky suggests they just sit and chill a bit while the corridors are empty, so that Quinn can get acclimated on this, his first day of school. They settle on a lobby bench with the dog lying beneath them.

Theirs is an easy companionship. But Becky, one of three veteran placement instructors managing these critical transitions, often makes a full confession to her students at the outset of their journey together: "I used to be afraid of blind people."

She was hopelessly uneasy with them when she first

started as a Fidelco volunteer, then as a kennel worker. When blind clients dropped by to pick up dog food orders or veterinary supplies, she would scuttle off on other business and let someone else take care of it.

"I was weirded out" is how she puts it. When she was asked if she'd like to become an apprentice trainer, she leaped at the chance; she loved dealing with the dogs, but not the clients, no thanks. Then she met a blind person who worked in the Fidelco offices. And Andrea Guidice—who also has a blind brother with a Fidelco dog—did not mind a bit when Becky screwed up the courage to pepper her with a fusillade of dumb-sighted-person's questions: How do you cook? How do you know how to put your outfits together? Put on makeup?

In the weeks it took Becky to go through her many questions, she and Andrea became friends. And to her own deep surprise, Becky found herself asking to go over to the human side of the Fidelco operation, to apprentice as a placement instructor. Instead of running from blind people, she'd be diving headlong into their lives, helping ease them through moments just like this.

She watches Eddie tense slightly as the bell shrills and doors are flung open for Quinn's first total teen immersion. Still lying on the floor, the dog raises his head calmly to face a roiling, jive-stepping sea of denim legs. Their clamor is mighty: squeaky sneakers, banging lockers, loud voices.

"Eddie, cool, you got the dog!"

"Ooooooh, Eddie, he's gorgeous, what's his name?"

The girls are instantly crazy for Quinn. Reaction from Eddie: a grin. From Quinn? Nothing. The dog is solid, serenely watching the passing parade just past his nose.

"Let's walk," says Becky, and they join the stream. No problem.

Quinn is practically a preteen in dog years, and Becky has found that young male shepherds can be a bit immature at this age. So she is smiling as he smoothly finds a path for Eddie—another preconception smashed. This boy dog is a mature gentleman. And he is pulling admiring teenagers toward Eddie like a lodestone. The trip to their next class is anything but lonely.

"It's interesting, the way people react in the hallway," Eddie is saying. "Some people are afraid of him. They think he'd attack even though he wouldn't hurt a fly. Some people yell at others when they try to pet him, 'Don't touch the dog!' It makes it more interesting—there's more options for things to go on. I like having him with me. It does help the confidence level."

It may sound like no big deal to some people, but it's "fairly major," Eddie says, to simply walk like a man, briskly, head up, no hesitation or tap-tapping. "It does give you that freedom. All you have to do is let your legs go. You can just put your trust in the dog and you're okay to go. You don't have to worry: you know they're not going to walk you into something. Yeah, it's a freedom thing."

On the whole, though, he's most eager for his own trip across the stage to snare the diploma. "High school is weird. People are changing constantly, so it's hard to say where you stand with them. I'm glad that high school is almost over. I like the people, but I almost feel the people will be easier to relate to once I'm in college. There's more of a variety, there's more acceptance, I guess."

Eddie's BrailleNote is full of poems; he says he has written two novels on it. He is mad for J.R.R. Tolkien books and the *Harry Potter* series. Even his screen name—a play on a Tolkien character—suggests a puff of dragon smoke. "I'm into creative writing. Fiction, poetry. Fantasy, anything along those lines."

Eddie is headed for Western New England College in Springfield, Massachusetts. He says he knew it was for him the moment he stepped on campus for a tour; it just felt right. He got his acceptance letter at the same time Courtney learned of her admission to graduate school. "Mom's crying. Of course. I didn't cry. But I'm glad that I'm going to be close. I never wanted to go far because I'm not the kind that likes to be far from home for a long time. You don't feel as rooted in other places. I'm glad I'm close, especially if there's a problem with Quinn. Fidelco is right there."

Thus far, there have been no difficulties with Quinn. Becky has gotten calls from Eddie on minor issues. "Quinn had a slight ear infection and I drove up with some medication. But they're solid in terms of behavior." Becky expects to be making the trip to Springfield to settle them into a new landscape. "I guess she'll come up and show me some mobility stuff around the college so that Quinn and I are both acclimated," says Eddie. "And he'll probably memorize the routes before I do."

Courtney is excited for all their futures—her marriage, her mother's, Eddie's first venture from home. "We're all splitting up, but in a good way. I think we maybe could have gotten here without the dogs—maybe. But I don't think I'd be the same person today without Meeka. She helped me open up a lot, become a lot more confident, a lot more responsible, and a lot more relaxed. I think you do have to relax a bit when you have any dog. You're going to be covered in dog hair, everything's not going to be clean all the time, there's going to be drool—and it's okay. Dogs need time to have fun, too. Taking care of someone else besides yourself, that automatically makes you a more responsible being. It's a two-way street."

She understands that Meeka is probably halfway through her working life now, but there is no way the family will part with her. If it's not feasible for her to stay with Courtney when a replacement dog arrives, Meeka will live with Marie, who cracks, "I'll never be an empty nester." Since 2006, Marie has been working to finish a college degree in psychology with a minor in criminal justice, and she is determined to have it done soon. When all dogs and children go their ways, she predicts, "I'll be a mess, of course. But I'm expecting only good surprises from now on."

And it has begun. At the end of his senior year in high school, Eddie Tabor startled his mother by informing her there was no time to lose in getting a last-minute tux rental. He had just asked a girl to the prom, she said yes, and it was only a week away. Was handsome Quinn going to be their escort? Marie wondered. A sly grin played across Eddie's face as he told his mother no, he would be leaving his dog with her that evening.

"This way, I get to hold on to her arm all night."

Smooth Eddie was clearly pleased with himself.

"And Mom?" he added. "I thought of that all by myself."

CHAPTER FOUR

MOMMY'S EYES

Vicky had been—metaphorically speaking—curling up, really becoming a shadow. She was becoming disconnected. From everything. But seeing Vicky walking down the street for the first time with a guide dog—with her head up and her shoulders square—I was stunned. I had this sense, this wild hope, that our lives were turning a corner.

—Eamonn Nolan, Vicky's husband

Room 20 on the second floor of Toronto's Gledhill Public School is a cheery, high-ceilinged old chamber bristling with new enticements for the children with learning difficulties who churn through here each day for help with reading and math. They bend to their work beneath the gaze of a giant green Shrek, a few colorful iterations of SpongeBob, and a tangle of vibrant art projects and plants. On one corner of the chalkboard is a short list of names, mostly boys, who have slipped into a few reportable behaviors: playground disputes, overly loud voices, lunchroom trespasses.

Around the room, posters offer suggestions for "What To Do When You Are Angry."

Ask yourself: How does my body feel?
Take three deep breaths.

Or one can ask Mrs. Nolan for permission to go and quietly brush her guide dog, Angus, who dozes through their lessons on his own rug in a corner. Angus accepts the ministrations of antsy, upset, or frustrated children who calm themselves by smoothing his long, fluffy coat. Angus is much better than any old time-out. His big dark eyes are wise and sympathetic. He never seems to mind if a child wakes him from a nap, and he endures their grooming efforts with a stoic grace.

But this morning, Angus is missing; his rug is occupied only by a plush stuffed German shepherd guide dog wearing a toy harness. One boy cries in his next class after he is told that Angus is gone for good. Another is here now with a shopping bag full of farewell goodies for Mrs. Nolan to send to Angus's new home: tennis balls, a bone, dog treats. "Something fun to give Angus," reads the note.

"Angus is the best," explains a boy named Eric. "It just made me feel good to walk in here and see him. They call this class special ed and sometimes that doesn't feel nice the way people say it. But Angus is special, too. Good special. Angus was ours—he belonged in our room. It kind of made me proud."

Vicky Nolan, who teaches supplemental reading and math to second through sixth graders, is navigating the corridors here with only her cane on this very difficult morning. Angus, with whom she has traveled the world as a champion rower on the Canadian Paralympic team, and who was known as "Mommy's eyes" to her two small children, is at this moment being driven to the new home arranged by a colleague of her husband, Eamonn, also a teacher. The retired guide dog adopted by the colleague's neighbor had just died, and the family is very happy to welcome Angus. They promise regular updates on his well-being.

Vicky is hitting her marks in the classroom this morning, handing out papers, listening to students read their calculations aloud, but she is visibly shaken by the parting. "Really, I just can't talk about it today," she says quietly. "It's too raw."

No one here at school is happy about Angus's departure. According to Vicky Nolan's co-teacher Leisa Lewis, this big patient dog was one of the most effective classroom palliatives she has ever seen. "You would not believe the change in atmosphere in this classroom since Angus joined us. The noise, the anxiety levels, and the acting out have all been lowered. He's just had such a calming effect. I would call him a very soothing presence."

Despite his valorous service, Angus had to be retired from guide dog service. He had become noisily anxious around other dogs, barking loudly at them, and was too preoccupied in their presence to function at his best. There are so many canines in the Nolans' nearby neighborhood that Vicky's daily walks to school had become an anxiety-provoking gauntlet. Attempts to correct his behavior with Fidelco instructors who came to Toronto were in vain. They recommended his retirement, but in the end, it was Vicky's decision. It is an excruciating loss, and this morning, everyone is acutely aware of the empty rug in the corner.

"Shall I start this for you?" Vicky is handing out a sheet of math problems to three boys who will solve them together. She uses a whiteboard, writing in large numerals, to demonstrate problems. They are barely visible in the narrow central vision she has remaining as her degenerative eye disease progresses. She was diagnosed at eighteen with retinitis pigmentosa, a condition that often begins with night blindness and can narrow sight to tunnel vision or complete blindness by one's forties or fifties. There are several forms of RP, with varying onsets and prognoses. No one else in Vicky's family has it, but her parents are both carriers of the gene.

As her vision has worsened, she has made adjustments with adaptive equipment, both low- and high-tech. "The whiteboards with large writing help," she says. "If the kids are doing their writing in their notebooks, I get them to read it back to me because I can't see it. I think it's good for them, too, to go back and read it out loud. Then they hear all their own mistakes." She also has a CCTV—a device that allows her to put a paper or book in front of a closed-circuit camera that magnifies it on a video screen. And her computer can take standard black type and display it as yellow type on a dark background, which is easier to see.

"I have that computer here at school, and I'm trying to get one at home. I'm also getting a great new CCTV. With the one that I have now, you're limited to sliding a book underneath, or a paper. This new one has a base and an arm with a camera attached that you can manipulate, so I can put my kids' toys underneath, or a food label. I can turn it around. It's very portable." She expects this will have many household applications. "If my kids are playing at the other end of the room, I can turn it toward them and see what they're doing. I'm excited that you can also turn it to your face. I'll be able to do my makeup."

No enhancement is needed; hers is a beautiful, unlined thirty-five-year-old face framed by lustrous dark hair. Her trim, strong body has been honed by hours in a racing shell on the river, training on the rowing machine—and keeping up with children. As her students set to their work, Vicky perches on a kid-sized chair and describes the current state of her disability: "I have enough vision that I can see my children if they're right in front of me. So I know what they look like. What vision I have is very central. They can't give me any further prognosis. It was pretty stable up until the birth of my kids, when I lost more. I'm hoping it'll be stable again. I'm also very hopeful there will be a cure. It's a stem-cell or gene therapy possibility."

Meanwhile, there will be another Fidelco shepherd. After school today, the instructor Jason Stankoski—known as Jay to his students—will meet her at home with Vegas, the dog that will replace Angus. Jay also trained Vicky with Angus, and before that, with her first guide dog, Jetta, who was also retired. To be partnered with one's third guide dog in just a few years is highly unusual. But Vicky's experiences illustrate the complexities and vulnerabilities of the human/dog bond.

The dogs' successions are also a result of Fidelco's ongoing follow-up to assess guide dogs throughout their working lives. Besides a standard observation six months after a dog's placement, all working guide dogs are evaluated yearly. "It can just be a phone call if the dog has been functioning well for a long time," says Jay. "But on-site visits are always good because an instructor may notice something that the student could not—maybe a chewed chair leg or upholstery fringe. We can provide simple behavior corrections to avoid problems in the future."

It was a routine check that turned up some issues with Jetta. "In terms of getting me around, Jetta was a very good guide dog," says Vicky. But sometimes a dog can care and protect too much; Jetta was so quickly and fiercely attached to Vicky that, instead of searching for an empty seat anywhere on a bus as she was taught, she would walk Vicky to the first seat up front and stare at its occupant until he or she got up and moved. During that check, a Fidelco instructor noticed that the dog also showed signs of stress at night; she appeared anxious and inclined to be overly protective of Vicky. Jetta was retired, and found another home as a pet. Nonetheless, Vicky found using a dog so transforming, she was eager for a replacement.

When Angus arrived, she visited all the classrooms with him and talked to the students about how he would be helping her. She discussed rules for student behavior; no petting, feeding, or playing when Angus is in harness and on the job. Recently, when she made the decision to retire him, she told only the students in Room 20, as they are the most affected.

"We had a discussion about getting the new dog," she says. "I haven't said anything yet to the rest of the students in the school, for a bunch of reasons. Yesterday it was really crowded with kids coming to say goodbye to Angus. And then today I was going to announce it—but I'm having a hard time dealing with it, actually. It's much harder than I thought. So I don't want to explain it to them all today. Obviously on Monday they'll notice that there's a new dog."

Her own children, son Tarabh (pronounced TA-rab), six, and daughter Ceilidh (pronounced Cayley), four, who adore Angus, took the news of his departure well, she thinks. "We love Angus," she and Eamonn had explained to them. "Angus was Mommy's eyes, but he's not Mommy's eyes anymore. Her new eyes are Vegas." They are excited to come home from kindergarten and day care today and meet Vegas—and they understand that they must keep their distance from this new family member at first, while he gets used to being special partners with Mommy.

Despite the difficulty in parting, Vicky says she will not miss the daily and growing anxiety of trying to navigate around other dog walkers with a barking, overprotective Angus. "Getting ready to leave the house, it's almost like getting ready to jump off a cliff. You've got to build up that courage, you're wondering, 'What's going to happen out there today? Who am I going to have to argue with?'"

Part of the problem, she believes, is that some people were afraid of Angus to begin with. "He weighs a hundred pounds. If he's barking, he looks really intimidating, even though he just wanted to sniff the other dogs. It wasn't aggressive at all. But a German shepherd's barking can invoke a scary stereotype to some people."

Even a perfectly behaved guide dog can draw startling responses on occasion. Vicky recalls one harrowing venture into the subway. "When you hear the door open, the command to the dog is 'find inside.' Then 'find a seat.' One of the first times I went in, even before I gave the command to find a seat, a woman was literally trying to climb the walls, she was so scared. She was crying and standing up on the seat. Things like that are just embarrassing for me. Even though she should be embarrassed."

If they only knew, she found herself thinking at such moments. Save for sounding off at other dogs, Angus is a gentle soul, especially with all the children surrounding him daily. "Angus has been amazing. My daughter was two when we got him and she would tug on his ears and lie on him, and he was very patient. When it got to be too much he just got up and walked away."

A good number of Fidelco clients have some form of retinitis pigmentosa, and received their dogs at varying stages of vision loss. The decline may be rapid or take place over many years. Vicky's onset was so gradual and insidious that she simply considered herself naturally clumsy. The woman who now has a sparkling set of sports medals on her dining room wall was always failing gym at public school in Pickering, a suburb of Toronto. "Growing up, I had all the regular checkups. I had glasses prescribed. So we never thought it was a vision problem. My family wondered, though. I knew I was clumsy and bumping into things and my parents thought they had been overprotective of me, that I hadn't learned how to look out for myself."

In hindsight, she realizes that there were some cues early on. "My first memory of the problem was in seventh grade being in a play, and we had to enter in the dark, through the auditorium, up the stairs onto the stage. And I couldn't figure out why no one else was having a problem with it. I had to hold on to the costume of the girl in front of me so I knew where I was going."

It was her fumbling in the dark that finally alarmed her parents. "When I was seventeen, I went out to a concert at night. When it was over, I went to step off the bleachers into what I thought was the aisle, and we were actually ten feet up in the air. My mom grabbed me. That's when she realized there was something seriously wrong."

The first doctor ignored her complaints about poor night vision and blamed astigmatism. The next diagnosed RP, but with few details or a prognosis. Now she thinks the gradual unfolding of a final diagnosis may have been a mercy. "I remember the look on my parents' faces, and I didn't really understand why they looked so devastated. I didn't get it right away. Then I was referred to yet another doctor, so I got little bits of information, six months to a year afterward. I think that helped me to deal with it, rather than getting hit with it all at once. Another doctor said, 'You shouldn't be driving.' I had done some research, and I found out that if you had less than twenty degrees of vision, you were considered legally blind. And then when I went to the specialist at the Hospital for Sick Children, she told me I had about ten degrees of vision. That really floored me."

As a new student at the University of Toronto, she spent her evenings out reliant on the vigilance of a trusted circle of friends. "When I started going out to nightclubs and movies, it was difficult. It got to the point that I'd only go out with certain people because I knew they would look out for me. I remember trying to go to the washroom on my own, and I got lost. I ended up in a corner touching the walls, thinking, 'I have no idea how to get out of here.' "

She had entered into the harrowing, often humiliating twilight stage between being able to "pass" as sighted and absolutely needing mobility assistance. "I tried to pass as much as I could," Vicky says. "I got the cane, but I would only pull it out when I really needed it. Even now my husband always tells me I'm trying to do too much, I'm trying to act like a sighted person. It's hard to give it up. Each time I've had to admit, 'Okay, I can't do *this* anymore,' it's been really hard."

Grappling with failing sight is an emotionally charged struggle; working it out in public only adds to the agony. "When I found out that I qualified for a cane, I wanted it right away. Not to help me physically get around, but so people would know. People had said to me, 'What's wrong with you, are you drunk?' I felt stupid."

Insensitivity was never an issue with Eamonn Nolan, the genial Irish Canadian fellow student who became her fiancé.

They were both destined for teaching careers in the Toronto public schools. "He's been with me through the diagnosis and everything," Vicky says. "But it never got in the way. When he told his family that he was going to propose to me, another member of the family said, 'You really need to think about this—she might go blind.' It made him really angry."

As she learned to cope with her growing visual impairments, Vicky went on to get her master's degree, and lectured in psychology at a city college, in addition to teaching second grade at Gledhill. Eamonn had landed a plum assignment teaching English and drama at a performing arts high school. Vicky felt almost in control of her life, and her disability—until they decided to start a family.

Vicky is home alone, with toddler Tarabh and infant Ceilidh, and it is not going well. The second childbirth has cost her more sight, and at home, the worry has doubled. Tarabh is jealous of his little sister, and Vicky cannot see or catch him as he swoops past the baby and delivers a petulant swat.

She is desperate to get all three of them out in the fresh air. It has been a struggle, but she has loaded them into a kiddie wagon; a stroller won't work because she can't see them beyond its canopy. She is hoping she can peer back at them in the wagon, and catch them in her narrow central field of vision. Maybe.

They bump down the front path and out to the sidewalk, where Vicky is trying to pull the wagon along with one hand and navigate with her cane in the other. The children's heads jounce as the wheels catch in snow piles and sidewalk cracks. Mittens drop and Vicky does not see them; woolen hats fall unretrieved in their wake. Now the baby is fussing, but she can't tell why.

She can feel tears coming as she turns the wagon around and heads for home. It's just not working. Nothing is working. Fumbling back into the house with Ceilidh clutched in one arm, Vicky is exhausted. She gropes along wiggly little bodies and unzips snowsuits and jackets, diapers the baby by practiced touch, and sinks down, defeated. All three of them cry for their own reasons, in the dark.

What to do? Vicky and Eamonn discussed getting a guide dog, but the schools they found required nearly a month's residential stay, with very limited or no family visits—impossible for two working parents whose children were so young. Then, through the school district's "vision team," which works with visually impaired students, they found out about Fidelco's on-site placement and applied.

Vicky had her first interview with Fidelco by phone, then shipped them a video made by one of Eamonn's students as a class project. The Fidelco training staff needed to assess her current mobility skills before making a decision and matching her with a dog. Given the distance, this was the most efficient way. They had received tapes from applicants before, but they were not expecting a music video.

Kachunka-BOOM!

The monster beat of urban hip-hop rumbles from the VCR deck as Dave Darr and Ron Labonte, Fidelco's director of training operations, settle in to assess applicant

Victoria Nolan's mobility skills. On the screen, Vicky walks confidently down a Toronto street, lightly holding Eamonn's arm. Her stride is brisk, and not at all tentative; now they're running together as the music builds.

Now they're pushing their two young children in a double stroller. The shot tightens to an arty close-up of stroller wheels and Vicky's sensible black brogans hitting the sidewalk in easy, uninterrupted cadence—no missteps. Cut to a playground swing set; Vicky is pushing Ceilidh in the baby swing, adjusting her little boot. Another close-up: a cane on the ground beneath the swings.

No, a passerby wouldn't catch her visual impairment at first, not with the fluid, natural way this mother moves, hoisting a baby out of the swing, handing her off, getting on a seesaw, all four of them now, up, down, up. She is smiling beneath dark glasses.

Vicky is striding along alone now, the rap lyrics are rhyming on about Sartre and Camus, and the cane seems synced to the beat, tap-tapping along the sidewalk ahead of her, past a junk shop, easing up curbs. She steps quickly and evenly down the subway stairs, back out again, now onto a bus, off the bus.

Vicky is on an escalator with Eamonn, moving off at the top without a hitch, now walking herself through traffic, careful to stop and listen, moving between pedestrians and storefronts, threading her way through an obstacle of bent metal bumpers, up a slope, back to the sidewalk.

Tight shot of Tarabh asleep in the stroller. Fade to black.

"She seemed fairly capable, and was a very aware cane traveler," Dave Darr recalls, "although I was concerned about finding a dog and a pace compatible with young walkers or a stroller. Away from the children, she stepped out well. So we needed to match her with a versatile-paced dog."

At the outset, Jetta was that. And Angus would prove an even better match for Vicky. "With a cane, I had to walk so slowly," she says. "Your brain was focusing so much on trying to figure things out. Then, once I got a guide dog, I was free to think about whatever I wanted and be able to just . . . walk. I could just give it over to the dog and let it lead. Oh, it was so liberating. I couldn't believe it. I hadn't walked that fast in years."

Maybe it was the wind on her face again; maybe it was the new freedom of movement. Vicky dared to look forward. She began searching for some sort of physical exercise that she could do. "I started rowing just four years ago. I don't know exactly how I came to it. I was looking for something active to do. I tried things that my friends were doing and I couldn't keep up with classes and all. The CNIB, the Canadian National Institute for the Blind, has a sailing program. I think that's what got me in mind of water sports. I thought, 'Sailing's not very active'—that's how I came to rowing. I just did a search of rowing in Toronto. The rowing club I now go to had a big article on their home page about how it was a good sport for those with disabilities. I knew it was something I'd be able to do, that I'd be supported and safe. Then I tried it and fell in love with it."

She got very good, very quickly; after just eighteen months on the water, she qualified for the Canadian Paralympic team's adaptive rowing LTA (legs, trunk, arms) "coxed four" event. In that category, the racing shell is crewed by two men, two women, and a coxswain with no disabilities. Their first major international event was the 2007 world championships in Munich.

They trained intensively on Lake Fanshawe in London, Ontario, two weeks prior to the event.

As it happened, this was also the time that Vicky had to transition between guide dogs. Jay drove Angus to Toronto, where they embarked on another kind of concentrated training. "It amazed me how quickly we bonded," Vicky says. "I got him when I was leaving for the world championships in just two weeks. So I knew that it had to be a quick bond in order for me to feel safe taking him to Germany. I think it took two days and I knew that I could trust him. We just got along. I don't know how it happened."

Angus has been left on the dock, in the care of waterfront staffers, and he is clearly anxious. He whines as Vicky climbs into the shell with the rest of her team. They are rowing away strongly, swiftly, as one, headed farther out on the lake. Angus has not taken his eyes off Vicky as the shell picks up speed and shoots out of sight.

Soon spectators on the dock are chuckling at a canine ritual repeated over and over as Vicky's shell makes circuit after circuit. Every time she comes within view, Angus rises, paces, whines. And whines some more. When they row out of sight, he settles into a morose posture, head on paws. When at last Vicky climbs back onto the dock, Angus strains to get to her. She can swear there is gentle rebuke in his anxious expression:

Where were you? Don't you know you need me?

Two weeks later, Angus and Vicky took their first flight across the Atlantic together with the team. They came home from Munich with the bronze medal and a very solid partnership. Reliving their time together on this tough first day of separation, Vicky unconsciously switches between past and present tenses as she describes how that bond deepened with Angus and the whole family: "He always needs to know where I am. If I would sneeze, he'd come over from wherever he was in the house, even if he was sleepy—you'd hear him dragging his feet, wanting to see if I'm okay. The kids would be sleeping, and if one of them coughed he'd go into their room, check on them, and come back to me as if to report they're okay."

She loved his sweet vigilance. And she admits that she may have tested the dog at first, since she still had the impulse to use what was left of her sight, occasionally second-guessing his directional pull. Jay saw some typical signs of resistance in Vicky in those first days of training. "You'll see the student looking off in a direction other than where the dog is going, or having a resistant body posture—a rigid right arm that should just be swinging naturally as they walk. I have to tell them that they're cheating the dog. If they don't trust it, the dog will stop offering its guide behavior."

Jay says this is a common tendency, but it can frustrate an eager young dog fresh from its training when its harness is continually bumped by the knee of a less-than-obedient human partner. Sometimes, Jay has his students with some remaining sight wear a blindfold until they can completely give control over to the dog.

"Relax—you'll just make him nervous," he told Vicky, adding that a person's anxiety can be transmitted down the leash and into the harness; a dog picks up easily on stress. Vicky acknowledges that anxiety has been one of the more overwhelming effects of her disability. Ask her about one of her greatest victories in overcoming it and she smiles. "It may sound silly. But it was a trip to the mall." She is referring to a huge complex in downtown Toronto known as Eaton Centre. It is the third-largest mall in Canada, with over 1.7 million square feet of retail space.

Close your eyes and imagine sightlessly navigating the diabolically designed retail rat maze that is your nearest shopping mall. Even a tube-sock kiosk can inflict terrors. "Whenever I would get near this mall, I would get so much anxiety I would have a hard time breathing," Vicky says of Eaton Centre. "It was almost like a panic attack just from going near it."

And so she put a mall walk on the list she made with Jay of things she would like to tackle during training with Jetta. Jay thought it prudent to repeat the exercise with the two successor dogs as well. He says he took his teams into it gradually each time. "We parked several blocks away in a more quiet area and worked on skills like pedestrian clearance. Navigating big crowds is hard. We worked our way in toward more congested areas, which took over an hour. Vicky was a champion working on her skill set there—stairs, obstacles like signs and kiosks, pedestrians, wheelchair ramps."

And in this new and complex obstacle course, the dogs found new permutations on the command "find the way." Vicky recalls, "It was just a feeling of giving that over to the dog—it was a weight lifted off. You completely have to trust the dog. It's letting go and letting the dog do the work for you. I walked from one end of the mall to the other, calmly. I didn't have to worry about bumping into anyone. People got out of my way. To go from that anxiety of not being able to breathe to just being able to walk calmly through. It was night and day—it was amazing."

It was with Angus—and Jay—that Vicky also found the courage and the motivation to challenge some of the discrimination she experienced as a guide dog user. It had happened plenty of times: refusal of service in a restaurant, cabdrivers who sped past her when they saw the dog. And at first, she was disinclined to argue her case with the perpetrators. It was infuriating and embarrassing, and her instinct was to withdraw.

"When I started having a lot of problems getting in places and hassles with the taxis, my husband starting driving me places more and picking me up. It's been hard on him. He was really worried because it was quite stressful for a while there. I think now I have a community of places where I'm known and there won't be an issue. I tend to go to those places. Every time I go to a new place, I have anxiety because I'm pretty sure there's going to be an issue. I've been fighting that for so long. It's been a problem here, and in terms of any enforcement of the law, it's been a slap on the wrist in the past."

She is grateful that she was not alone when yet another cab-driver refused to let her and Angus get into his vehicle. "We were training. Jay had already gotten in when the driver refused to let me in, so Jay could get all the information. A lot of people can't follow up because they're not able to see enough to get the license plate. It's happened to me before—where the cab will slow down and when they see the dog, drive away, and there's nothing I can do to follow up."

Armed with a witness and the driver's name and license number, Vicky filed a complaint. When the case came up in court, Jay, who was in the midst of placing two dogs in Lansing, Michigan, juggled his schedule with his students there and drove all night, over eight hours, to appear as a witness. "He slept for two hours in his van outside our house," Vicky says. "We had to testify separately, with the other person out of earshot. But of course our stories matched. The driver was found guilty of breaking the law and fined $2,000. Then he had to appear before the taxi tribunal, and they took his license. So this was good. Not that it's setting a precedent, but it's helpful just to get the message out." When she and the driver were left alone together momentarily in the courtroom, he was unrepentant about refusing her service. But in a strange disconnect, he did tell Vicky, "I feel sorry for you."

The experience was galvanizing. And she has grown more steadfast in challenging those who refuse her access. "We had trouble in Miami when we were training for the Paralympics. There were hotels that would not let us in. There were two that said outright that we couldn't stay and one that wanted five hundred dollars to steam-clean the room when we were gone. We've followed up on those as well. We're just asking that they train all their employees and put up a sign that service dogs are welcome. We really just want to educate people."

The problems continue, and it nettles her. "For me, I just want to go about my business and not have to justify why I'm there."

To her surprise, she has found herself comfortable and willing to speak in public about her more positive experiences. "Speaking was always something that I hated, even in front of my class. And now I'm starting to go out and speak to large groups of people. For an audience of kids, I'll talk about overcoming obstacles, about how you can accomplish anything. I also like to tell them that rowing is a sport where you use mostly your legs to move the boat and that we have athletes who competed in the Paralympics who don't have use of their legs—they make it work with arms only. I speak to adults as well. So many people come up to me later and say how inspiring it was. That feels great."

So much has happened with the help of these dogs—a new freedom, her globe-trotting athletic career. She has pushed the limits imposed by her own disability and she has learned a good deal about the hurdles others face—and overcome. She sees it in her rowing teammates. "I'm the only one with a visual impairment," she says. "The other woman was born with some sort of birth defect and she doesn't have all her fingers. So she has to have her hand strapped to the oar. One man had his leg amputated in an accident and the other had a spinal cord injury. He was one of the top triathletes in the country and was hit by a truck on a bike ride."

All of them managed rigorous training as well as constant individual time trials to keep their place on the team. Eamonn recalls a very anxious time for Vicky as the Paralympic games neared. Hard training had produced a blood clot in one arm, and she was taking blood thinners to dissolve it when another challenge surfaced. "She found out there was a seventeen-year-old in British Columbia who was pulling extremely fast times and wanted her seat on the boat in Beijing," he says. "So Vicky had to start training on blood thinners, getting bruises like you wouldn't believe, to compete against this kid half her age. I'd drop her off at the hospital and Angus would lead her into the hospital, she'd get her blood test, Angus would lead her to a cab, she'd go to work, then Angus would lead her around to the club and she'd row. Then she had to go and race this woman in person at a training center in London, Ontario. I drove her there with Angus—it's a four-hour drive. And I have this image of Angus taking her to her room."

On the first day of trials, the challenger beat Vicky—badly. Eamonn says she called home crying. "I had to say, 'You're on your own, Vick. I can't help you.' But I know the dog did. Angus was there with her for those trials and tribulations. She had someone to pet and cuddle. She went back the next day and blew that girl out of the water. Could any of that really have happened without Angus? I don't think so, I really don't."

Having fought off the challenge for her seat, Vicky moved on to the hard part. "Before Beijing, my schedule was crazy," she recalls. "I would be up and out of the house by 5:15, and down to the rowing club, which is at the other end of the city. I would train for an hour and a half, come back home, shower, run to school, work all day. Then my trainer would come to school and we did weight training here at the end of the day. I'd go home and eat and head back to the club for a second row at night."

The punishing routine paid off. The team qualified to represent Canada. Angus managed the eleven-hour flight from Vancouver to Beijing with no problems. As he had for the Munich trip, Jay provided detailed advice on reduced feeding and water before the flight, how to enlist sympathetic gate agents for help in relieving the dog on the tarmac, and passing through security. In these jittery times, security personnel may insist on X-raying a dog's harness or taking a hair sample to test for possible residue from explosive chemicals.

Once they rested and headed out into the Olympic Village, Vicky made an amused entry in the "Diary from Beijing" she e-mailed to colleagues and friends:

> The funniest thing has been the reaction to Angus. Not only because he's a guide dog, but because he's so big! There are volunteers EVERY-WHERE you go and every time I go somewhere new

they all crowd around me (20-30 people) and all start taking photos of Angus and oohing and aahing over him. It's hilarious. I have a picture of people taking pictures of him just because it is so crazy. It's like paparazzi, there are flashes going all the time. And I generally have an entourage of volunteers around me as I'm walking just because of Angus. . . .

It is so interesting to see so many different disabilities and how other countries support them. For example, today we saw an athlete who is a double leg amputee and he walks on them—he has wooden boards under his leg to assist but no prosthetics. It's amazing.

We went to Shunyi today, the rowing venue, and rigged our boat. . . . I had to be back early to get classified by a doctor (to make sure I am still visually impaired!!) and he certified my blackout goggles to make sure no light gets in. I still find it funny that everyone else has adaptations to improve their disability while mine is made worse by blocking out the little vision I have left.

So that's day one in Beijing. Overall a little overwhelming but very well organized and very beautiful.

I'm feeling so proud to be here!

Despite all the Chinese hosts' attention to detail in the Olympic Village, Vicky was hardly prepared for the thoughtful and overwhelming embrace of disabled athletes that awaited them at the opening ceremonies, which were held in the same "Bird's Nest" stadium built for the 2008 Summer Olympics. On September 6, 2008, with special permission to admit a dog, she and Angus took their places in the line of march behind the Canadian flag. Standing there, holding the leash and harness, she was stunned by the spectacle—and thrilled that Eamonn was there to share it with her.

Far from being staged as an afterthought or a lesser version of the regular Olympics, this was a lavish celebration of the possible, the probable, and the downright heroic. "Everything was just so moving and beautiful," Vicky recalls. "For the lighting of the flame, a woman athlete came out with her guide dog—she was the first woman to win a gold at the Paralympics for China. She passed the flame to a Chinese athlete in a wheelchair, and he hoisted himself up a rope to the top of the Bird's Nest—with the wheelchair. The flame was attached to the wheelchair, and he lit the flame at the top. It was incredible."

She stops, and flashes a big, easy smile at the memory. "I never imagined a disability could get me somewhere amazing like that—especially for sports. It's so funny because I was always failing gym class and didn't know why."

Vicky and her team did not medal this time, but she says the experience was its own reward. "And we'll be back to try again!" When they packed for the journey home, Eamonn included a long metal cylinder encircled by Chinese characters—a torch. He was chosen to be part of the torch relay, and helped carry the flame for all the Paralympians, including the woman he calls "my beautiful, amazing wife."

Family members who have had a Fidelco shepherd partner with their visually impaired loved one—husbands, wives, children, parents—have traveled long and often difficult journeys themselves. Most family members are voluble about the positive changes in their households once a guide dog becomes part of it. They are also blunt and honest about the adjustments they must make to welcome a furry new family member with its own needs into their lives and to provide a setting where it can function in top form.

Few family testimonials are more painfully direct—or more eloquent—than that of Eamonn Nolan, a tall, easygoing, and committed educator whose smile flashes gold, owing to a life-long hockey habit, and whose bookcase embraces titles as diverse as a text on medieval warfare and the punk manifesto *Please Kill Me*. His life with Vicky—call it "Love in the Time of Vision Loss"—has been fraught with unexpected peaks and valleys. Today presents one of those tough high/low moments, charged by the departure of one dog and the arrival of the next.

By early evening, the day has proved long, exhausting, and emotional. Eamonn has taken off from work to resettle Angus in his new home, tidy the house for the Fidelco instructor's arrival, and pick the children up from day care while Vicky and Jay test-drive Vegas. Most of his allotted vacation and personal days are spent on such necessities; since Vicky cannot see enough to safely measure medicine, he has had to skate off the hockey rink where he bangs sticks in a league of over-thirty doctors, teachers, and businessmen to drive home and administer a dose of Tylenol to a fevered child.

Clearing the table for a sit-down, Eamonn gestures toward the rest of the fairly tidy kitchen. "If there's a mess in the house,

Vicky can't see it," he says. "It's on me. Imagine—living with a man in charge of cleaning up." He laughs.

Hungry children are in and out of the kitchen pleading their case for a pizza supper as Vicky, Vegas, and Jay confer in the dining room. Eamonn has just calmed a fretful class parent on his cell phone ("Your son is a great kid, you know that. We just have to keep the gangbangers away from him"). The parents of all his students are welcome to his cell number. Since he requested a transfer from the rather cushy performing arts high school and landed—also at his request—in a struggling school in a poor urban area, his wife says that he comes home more tired—and far more satisfied with his day's work. He still teaches English and drama, and works with some students whose own lives play like Shakespearean epics of privation, immigrant isolation, and sporadic gang warfare.

He fell in love with Vicky at the University of Toronto— when she was still sighted enough to have her learner's permit for a driver's license. He married her after the devastating diagnosis, and watched her sight slip more with both childbirths. He has been both appalled and exhilarated by the turns their life has taken: "You can't imagine what it felt like carrying that torch through Beijing."

Theirs has been such an improbable journey. But Eamonn says that until now, he has never really sat down and talked about the miracle of the dogs, and how it has lifted his wife from a darkness that enveloped them all, and threatened to scuttle their happiness. Hearing him deliver what amounts to an extemporaneous soliloquy of despair and thanksgiving, it's clear he is thinking aloud, and many of the memories are tough to revisit. He is weary-looking but often smiling as he unspools it, forcing himself to go back to what he calls the "predog" days:

"It was such a dark time, literally and metaphorically. It was rough. Until we had kids, everything was manageable. Blindness was manageable, walking with a cane was manageable—we just were in a routine.

"When Tarabh came, you know, the trumpets blared— hallelujah, the baby! You just focus on him, and it's a real diversion from the vision degeneration. But after delivery, there was a pretty significant sight loss. We don't have a real way of measuring. It's just little things. We didn't go to the movies anymore, and Vicky watched less and less television. I notice that she didn't read, she didn't write on her computer—which is not like her.

"So things were different, but it became routine. Then when she got pregnant with Ceilidh, the doctor said something to the effect of: 'You should know that if you proceed with this pregnancy, you may go completely blind or lose a very substantial chunk of your vision.' I remember sitting with Vicky and talking about it early in the pregnancy. Saying 'What do you want to do?' She just decided, 'Okay, let's just do it.' What else can you do—was she going to have an abortion or something? No.

"So when baby number two came, we realized, 'Oh, we're in trouble.' As much as I extol the virtues of the health care system here, it really was a letdown for us when we realized we make too much money to get help and not enough money to pay for help. So we're middle-class people with two kids. And Mom's at home in the dark. When you have two babies and they're screaming and crying, you confront the reality of what is not possible anymore. Vicky was getting a piddling amount of maternity leave and I was working away, and we realized we'd better hire somebody. We hired a college student who came for half a day, every day, to help Vicky out, and it cost quite a lot.

"Then we realized we needed to hire someone full-time to look after the kids because Vicky just couldn't do it. So she was forced to go back to work prematurely because we couldn't afford to pay for child care without her being employed. In our house, there isn't a lot of room for self-pity and 'Woe is me.' No matter how much she cried, the situation wasn't going to change. So we just sort of accepted it.

"We ended up hiring the daughter of a colleague of mine, who was really the best possible nanny to have. We have an apartment we rent out, and we gave it to her. It cost a lot. And then we realized Tarabh was old enough for junior kindergarten. We could put them both into the same day care program. I think that was the worst, when Vicky saw that we had to put our children in day care and relinquish control of our children. Day care would never be my first choice. Maybe I could have taken the time, but I really don't have the strength to deal with it. I have vision and I can't do it. So we had to give up caring for them at home. It was a very expensive, very depressing, sad time. Because we were realizing that yet again, Vicky's disease had changed how we have to live life.

"That's when Vicky was at her lowest. I know she says it was when she was home alone with the kids in the dark, going blinder. But I think the real dark time was later, when she had to go back to work and she encountered a huge amount of prejudice. At school, an administrator said to her, 'We're going to put you in special ed.' Previously she had taught grade two. Vicky asked why and the administrator said, 'You have special needs, so wouldn't you be more comfortable working with kids with special needs?'

"Initially, Vicky really resisted that and was really upset about it. Then she went on to sort of accept it. Vicky was assigned to a classroom where the kids needed diapering and had seizures. One student with violent tendencies would punch Vicky around the face. She couldn't defend herself because she couldn't see it coming. Day after day.

"That was a bleak period, coming home to this pain and injustice. If your partner is beaten down in any way, it's really hard. And with children, you have to be stoic. We can't sit around crying and feeling bad. You have to give them dinner or take them to the playgroup and move on.

"Add to all this the fact that there's a terrible disease eating away at her sight and that she spends a little more time in the dark than you and I do—like ninety percent of her time is in darkness. She's in a dark world where things magically appear and hit her in the head or in the leg. There was a time before the dogs when she would use her cane at work and she'd come home with bruises like saucers on her leg because a kid would move a chair. Those things are hard to deal with, but ten times harder when you have children and you have to put them first.

"In that bleak time, there was no help, there was no guide dog. It was just 'Wow, this is how disabled people live.' It was a crash course. Vicky's blindness was a real eye-opening experience for me. It's a devastating and crippling experience to go blind. It's lonely, isolating. It's changed our social lives, it's changed our family life, it's changed how I view my job and Vicky's. It takes over everything. I still find myself discovering new ways that it's hellish. But in recent years, we've almost achieved balance."

Cielidh runs into the kitchen to present a final argument for a pizza delivery; Eamonn sends her back to Vicky with a terse directive: "Tell your mother I consider it a very good plan." He is smiling again, and ready to take his dark tale into the light, to a place where the bruised, depressed Vicky sheaths herself with the muscle and discipline to become a world-class athlete, to travel the world. He returns to the dogs.

"Now things are amazing. The arrival of the dog changed everything. Everything. The rowing is good, don't get me wrong. But I think the rowing is connected to the guide dog, I really do. Jetta and Jay came before her rowing. I don't know if Vicky would agree with this, but I think the experience of getting a guide dog indirectly led to her rowing. I credit the dogs, and Jason Stankoski.

"Right away, when Vicky got her first dog, Jetta, I could see a change in the way the world perceived her. First of all, the guide dog makes Vicky talk more, which is good. A lot of people don't realize that one of the symptoms of blindness is mutism. You stop being included; people stop talking to you. You stop existing.

"People don't pay attention to you when you can't see them. They think if you're blind, there's something else wrong with you. I watched people, even friends, ignore Vicky and tune her out. But the guide dog makes them aware. They seem to think, 'Oh, part of her can see. The furry German shepherd part can see what I'm doing.' And that's the part that people pay attention to."

The phone has begun to trill again—a hockey friend. There is a big, basso bark from the next room. Eamonn smiles, throws his arms wide in a gesture of mock surrender, and brings his narrative to its quiet but upbeat close:

"When Vicky first worked with Jay and her guide dog Jetta— that week or ten days changed her forever. It's just a new way of doing things. She's not back to who she was before she went blind—she's a new person with a new skill set and a new approach to life, which I think is good. I see that in all of us. Like when I changed jobs, I redefined myself. Well, Vicky's way of getting around has radically changed.

"It's such a good partnership. Whoever came up with this idea of a guide dog deserves the Nobel Prize. You realize why people say it's man's best friend, because the dog partnership is so strong. People see her coming with this magnificent animal and it's very empowering for Vicky. Consequently, for me as her husband, I feel like, 'Wow, now my wife can go to the park with the kids. And if my wife wants to go grocery shopping, she can do that.'

"I can't articulate the feeling I had when I realized we went from that phase of 'you can't' to 'you can.' It's been really good. Just knowing that Vicky can get up and out and be a normal part of society, it's been the weight of the world off my shoulders. It had gotten to the point that I was having panic attacks, which I had never really had, just tons of anxiety. I was so worried about her. That's gone with the dog."

Wrrrrruff. Vegas lets out a tentative bark as the doorbell rings.

"Another really important thing I wanted to say: Vicky has slowed us down in so many ways. And that's the best thing that she's done. Her blindness has made us move slower so we see more. We've relaxed our pulses. I'm grateful."

The pizza has arrived; a family dinner ensues—the Nolans, Jay, and now Vegas, who is lying under the table at Vicky's feet. Ceilidh is asked what she thinks of Mommy's new eyes.

"He's pretty. And big."

And from Tarabh: "Hey, Jay? Will you tell us when we can pet him?"

Jay has known the children now for most of their young lives. Watching their easy interaction from the kitchen doorway, Eamonn says, out of their earshot, "You can't really talk about this without considering Jay's contribution to our family life. It's incredible to meet someone who not only understands all of Vicky's disease issues but understands the detailed family and work arrangements you have to make in order to work with a dog. What a relief—what a weight off my shoulders."

When the Nolans retire for the night, Jay will go back to the less-than-lavish hotel room dictated by a frugal per diem allowance, and if it is not too late, he will call his five-year-old son, who has wondered, more than once, why Dad always has to toss a bag in the van and skedaddle—sometimes on a moment's notice if a client needs help. Like all Fidelco placement specialists, Jay can be gone three weeks at a stretch. And when he returns, it is often to the dreaded question, "Daddy, can't you stay home with me?"

Any parent who travels for work has labored over an acceptable answer. Jay has explained more than once why he must be away. Helping people with problems is something a kindergartener can understand, he thinks. Fidelco dogs are in and out of their home as he prepares for placements. One client's guide dog stays with the Stankoskis every summer. The man, who is Egyptian, returns to that country yearly, but has found it to be inhospitable to guide dogs. Kenneling that long would seriously compromise the dog's well-being and skills. "Why should he give up using a dog for the rest of the year?" Jason says. "It's no big deal to help him out."

Such is the difference between a job and a true vocation. In his previous line of work as an engineer, Jay was having a difficult time justifying his long, sometimes tedious road trips, even to himself. He specialized in teaching workers how to use new manufacturing equipment safely and more efficiently and helped standardize tool setups and fine-tune installations. It might mean a couple of weeks at the John Deere facility in New Mexico. Or a fateful assignment in New York City, where the apathy and wise-guy attitude of his trainees left him sitting morosely by a bridge in Astoria, Queens, when Dave Darr walked by with a guide dog in training. Man and dog looked happy with life. Jay had been training hunting dogs since he was a teenager in rural Connecticut, and the two men got to talking. Dave gave him his business card. And since he joined Fidelco on December 2, 2002, working his way from apprentice to trainer to placement specialist, Jay has never looked back "except with great relief."

Of course, there are bad days. The hardest task, any trainer will attest, is the rare case when he or she must remove a dog from a home. Dave Darr accompanied Jay on one such sad mission, but insisted that Jay take the lead in order to learn to handle such situations. They went to an assisted-living facility where a man in his late thirties, a stroke victim, had seen his condition deteriorate to where he was bedridden and would never be able to work the dog again. He wept when Jay reached for the leash.

"Please don't take my dog."

Gently, Jay explained. It was best for the dog, which was young and in need of regular exercise and work. And there was the unspoken imperative: another visually impaired person on the waiting list could reclaim independence by being paired with the animal. The man's father, a visibly grieving gentleman in his seventies, took Jay aside in the corridor and told him,

"You don't know what it's like, to have a child die before you do. Before he should."

Jay took the dog, but left deeply shaken. "That dad just crushed me."

Despite such excruciating scenarios, the job does offer consistent, if unorthodox, fringe benefits, including the chance to witness small, often unexplainable miracles. Jay cites his experience with a young woman in Michigan, a PhD student in neuroscience, who had fought back from a brain aneurism and surgery that resulted in devastating complications, including vision loss and the onset of diabetes.

They were training with her new guide dog when it suddenly crossed in front of her and blocked her path, refusing to go on despite commands of "forward" and a sharp correction. The dog would not let her take a step. Seconds later, she was in a near-faint from insulin shock. "Wow," she said as she sipped some fruit juice and recovered. "I had no idea that was happening."

"We didn't really put it together until a couple of days later," Jay recalls. "We were working in a mall, on an escalator, when the dog did the same thing—just put its body in front of her. She started to slump. I held her up until I could get her off the escalator and she began to have a petit mal seizure. Then the dog was licking her face—as if to try to bring her around." The dog was alert to both insulin shock and the seizure—the woman's first. Her seizures have continued, along with diabetes-induced problems. But her guide dog continues to warn her of both with its own spin on "intelligent disobedience."

It is always gratifying to see a dog progress beyond its training and offer helpful behavior on its own. "These dogs are so physically attuned to a person," Jay says, "and they're just so smart. In every placement, I'll see them do something that shows they're totally on the beam. And every time, it stops me cold and makes me think, 'Oh, my God.'"

After a few days in Toronto, Vegas is working well, moving calmly and briskly from home to school to rowing practice. He is well behaved in the presence of other dogs and unfazed by his first plane trip, a short hop to Montreal. He proves himself to be a gentleman when he assumes his place in Room 20; the Gledhill students are delighted to see him, though a few are confused:

"Holy cow—Angus got a haircut!"

Around the house and out of harness, there is a bit of "terrible two" about him as he races around, upending the occasional drinking glass or child. "The children love him," Vicky says. "He's very young, and he'll calm down. We're working on it."

Vegas had a short sojourn back in the Fidelco kennels when Eamonn surprised Vicky with a family trip to his parents' farm in Ireland. Special documentation for Vegas could not be completed in time, despite exceptions to the UK's strict quarantine procedures for service animals. In such circumstances, guide dogs can be boarded at Fidelco without charge, provided clients see to the dog's transportation there and back.

Unpaid and unbidden, Jay drove to Toronto to get Vegas and bring him to the Fidelco kennels. But he first kept the dog for a week in his own home so that he could give Vegas a few etiquette lessons about cruising kitchen countertops. Jay's going the extra mile—or seven hundred—is something the Nolans will never take for granted. Vicky says, "He continues to amaze us with his dedication and friendship."

Before they left for Ireland, Vicky had more good news. Despite persistent challenges for her seat on the rowing team by the same girl from British Columbia, Vicky had persevered. "I've made the Paralympic team again and we've been rowing gold-medal times. I feel like I'm in the best shape ever—and we're really training hard."

With Vicky's help, Eamonn has started a rowing club for his inner-city pupils, some of whom have never dared try a team sport. They row at the facility where Vicky trains. "A few of them are good enough to try out for the national team," she says. "We tell them to go for it. Who says they can't?"

CHAPTER FIVE

MADAM COMMISSIONER

The geneticists all wanted to study us—it must have been hundreds of doctors that we saw. We had many years of tests and sitting in dark rooms for hours, having our eyes dilated and patched. None of them had seen anything like us.

—Janet LaBreck

A city-smart dog is suave, even in a snowstorm. Here in Boston, at the onset of a nor'easter that is grounding planes at Logan Airport and causing car tires to whinny and spin on Boylston Street, two-year-old Osbourne is blazing a deft path through slush and ice at a pace even sighted persons might find daunting. His speed is no problem for Janet LaBreck, who is clipping along easily at his side through the winter mess, despite the chic three-inch heels on her knee-high boots.

Icy, pelting snow is frosting Osbourne's dark muzzle. He is a big, powerful animal on a mission: lunch. He hesitates at the door of one restaurant, a favorite of Janet and her husband, Russell.

But she urges him past it. Chinese today, please. Osbourne pads dutifully to the Asian lunch spot where this working woman—Commissioner Janet L. LaBreck, heading the Massachusetts Commission for the Blind (MCB) for the administration of Governor Deval Patrick—is welcomed warmly along with Russell, and they are shown to their regular table. Osbourne folds himself unobtrusively beneath it.

The LaBrecks are able to lunch together often; Russell works a floor above his wife at the MCB. As a rehabilitation counselor, he helps people who are newly blind find support and rehabilitation services. The three of them drive into the city daily from their rural home an hour west, unless Janet is traveling, which she does often as advocate-in-chief for the 36,000 visually impaired citizens of Massachusetts. The first person to hold the post was Helen Keller, who joined the commission in 1906.

Janet's rise to the top of the commission where she has worked for twenty-five years necessitated her getting a guide dog; she lost most of her sight to retinitis pigmentosa as a preteen and relied on a cane for most of the ensuing years. "When I was appointed as commissioner in 2007, I knew that my travel experiences were going to really increase and be pretty demanding," she says. "And my vision had diminished to the point where I knew I'd have to have more help. Even though I'm a very good cane user, I was going to be on airplanes and in different cities, so I felt that using a guide dog would be best for me."

Russell is smiling as he tucks into his spicy chicken. "I knew she would be much safer traveling with a dog," he says. "So it was a great relief to me. And I'm just crazy about Osbourne. Feel free to stop me anytime I gush about his more miraculous qualities." Russell had already seen the advantages of a guide dog.

Together twenty-five years, he and Janet met in college and had been married for nearly five years when she got her first Fidelco dog, a long-haired female named Xippy (pronounced Zippy), in December 1991. The dog's photo is still on the wall in Janet's office. She explains that Xippy was an excellent guide dog. The sense of freedom she conferred was miraculous. And it was very difficult to give her up, but she had no choice.

"I had a chronic illness as a result of a surgery gone wrong. I suffered from acute peritonitis, and I was ill for about three years. I didn't have the strength or stamina to effectively use the dog. So they placed her with somebody who could—a teacher. I used cane travel all the intervening years."

Janet listens to arriving diners stomping the snow off their shoes and is reminded of just how she was trained for New England days such as this: "When I got Xippy, it was in a major blizzard. I was in West Springfield and I was sure we weren't going out and here was my Fidelco trainer at the door. He goes, 'This is the best time to work to navigate the snow piles.'"

That was John Byfield, who instructed her with both dogs. He says that Osbourne was carefully chosen to meet the requirements of her new position: "Janet is an active person: she travels extensively. Once a month she's on the road, to California or down south. She needed a dog that was energetic but capable of switching off and being quiet when she was in meetings. And she needed one that was very comfortable around other dogs because at the agency there are many other guide dogs."

In fact, there was guide dog gridlock in the corridor and ladies' room as Janet left the MCB for lunch. Osbourne, perhaps preferring the additional space, always leads Janet straight to the handicapped stall in restrooms. And he is on his best behavior with other dogs, even on nearby Boston Common, where they walk frequently for exercise and to keep Osbourne's city skills sharp.

"Janet is a good walker," observes John. "She walks around a track close to her home with her husband. She is a very self-sufficient, capable woman, and I think she's achieved a lot without having a dog. But having him makes it easier." He has worked with Janet in the city and the country. Not surprisingly, their most intense training was in urban settings. "The average dog can adapt to the country quite well—it's not taxing," John says. "They follow the left-hand side of the street, they alert to the intersection, it's not as heavy a workload as there is in the city. Dealing with traffic in Boston . . . well, Boston drivers are lousy. During the training, we also went to Bradley Airport outside Hartford, where she usually flies from, and worked around there and the hotel. There just happened to be a beauty competition for children. So we went in there and sat and Osbourne was very well behaved. There was lots of activity and little ones, and there was music going on. We tried to prepare him and her for as much as we could possibly think of. And it seems to be working well."

Janet was always conscious of having to earn her guide dog. "The commitment is twenty-four/seven," she says. "It's not the same as coming home at the end of the day and folding your cane up. I think that Fidelco looks for individuals who have that level of commitment and the seriousness about what it's going to entail. Second, they look for someone who is a good traveler, who is going to be out with the community. They want to know that you're going to be putting the dog to good use, you're not just sitting stagnant in the house all the time. The dogs are very high energy, they're young, and so they require a lot of work and exercise."

Robbie Kaman has bred her dogs to serve, but she insists they be respected and cared for in turn. Placement instructors must be vigilant about a dog's living conditions, family dynamics, and any undue stress. In extremely rare cases, Fidelco trainers have removed dogs who were being improperly cared for. The very worst day a trainer can have, says John, is having to take a dog from a client no longer strong or well enough to work with it—as with Janet and Xippy.

"Her primary consideration was for the dog," he says of that unhappy time. "And she gave her up knowing someone else could put her to fullest use." Having supervised Osbourne's selection and placement, John has found Janet to be the most conscientious of handlers, deeply attuned to the dog's needs and careful to ensure that he has plenty of exercise and constant reinforcement of his skills. They are a familiar sight walking crisply along the Common, and navigating some of the most hair-raising pedestrian crossings in urban America. Osbourne will remain a keen and energetic guide, John is sure, owing to the can-do outlook of his partner. "She's got a lot of spirit, drive, and capability. Her glass is always half full."

Back in Janet's large, airy office at MCB, Osbourne settles in for a snooze between deployments. Her job is rapid-paced and tightly, highly scheduled. She handles it with adaptive software, keen discipline, and an assistant named Antonio "Tony" Harris, who juggles a chorus of shrilling, beeping cell phones and Black-Berrys, drives her between the commission's other offices state-wide, and helps coordinate public appearances, such as her recent filming of a joint public service spot with the Boston Celtics about literacy through Braille. Janet also teaches case management and a graduate-level course in rehabilitation of the blind at Assumption College in Worcester. Her courses are given at night, after a long day on the job. She says that she is continually surprised at how comfortable and energized she now feels at the front of a classroom.

"I never saw myself as ever being a teacher. It was probably going back to my experiences being teased by kids in school. I never really saw myself as being able to stand up in front of a classroom and talk about my vision loss and try to present myself as an expert in the field. Getting over the anxiety wasn't easy. Over the years, I've had to relax and get comfortable with it, get comfortable with the students. And it's probably been one of the most rewarding fields I've had a chance to work in."

She thinks it's a good idea to talk about that anxiety, a constant companion for so many years. Janet has temporarily stilled all her clamoring electronics—sent them out of the room with Tony—as she settles in to retrace the unlikely path that brought her here. The obstacles she faced were invisible, but formidable. Worry, fear, and a Pandora's box of constant, hectoring insecurities can all be crippling side effects of vision loss and other disabilities. Janet can stand up before a convention hall of thousands and address those specters now. But in the late sixties, finding herself so suddenly different and so dependent was a crushing burden—especially for a young African American girl from a large, struggling family in a small New England city.

"People will often ask me which is worse, to lose vision as a child or as an adult. As a child, probably the one protection I had was that I didn't recognize that I was losing my vision. When you're a child with a progressive disease like this, as odd as that might sound, it's true—you don't get it right away. You automatically begin compensating even though you may not be aware of it."

Growing up in Pittsfield, Massachusetts, Janet loved sports. As she began to experience the erosion of her night vision, typical of RP, it became more difficult to snag pop flies and chase down a moving target in a game of tag as the sun began to sink.

"I would often say, 'You know what? It's getting dark, we should stop playing now.' I never thought that the kids thought that was weird—'What does she mean, it's getting dark? We can still see.' They would just listen to me. So I never realized that they were not having the same problem that I was. Children are so flexible. Adults have a tendency to just stop doing what they're having trouble with. Kids will always try to find another way."

It worked—until it didn't. She began to suffer the night terrors of people with progressive RP, the dreaded moments after dusk when the visual world dims and winks out, when familiar rooms seem to change dimension. Furniture barks shins and raises cruel bruises. And finally, schoolwork is rendered all but impossible. When she could no longer focus clearly on the blackboard, Janet's worried parents sought an expert opinion.

> *She doesn't think she likes this place. To a ten-year-old who has just made a long car trip across the state from her home in Pittsfield, the waiting room at Massachusetts Eye and Ear Infirmary in Boston is even more unsettling than the anxiety that descends every night now when the sun sets. All around Janet in the big, sterile space, people sit wearing eye patches, or blinking back drops as they wait for their eyes to dilate for examination. One after another, they are called away by white-coated doctors until it is her turn:*
>
> *"Janet Babbs."*

The doctor stands a distance away from her, holding an eye chart.

"I want you to read this for me."

The hand she holds over her right eye begins to tremble as she strains to recognize even the largest row of letters. Finally, she breaks the long, awkward silence.

"I can't see it."

Behind her, Elzie Babbs and his wife, Evelyn, watch with growing apprehension. Their oldest daughter is deaf and blind; Janet is their second child, and there are four more behind her. Despite two working parents, there is never enough money, and given the difficulties in just getting here—all the children had to cram into the car—there is certainly no time for nonsense.

"You'd better stop fooling around," Elzie growls, "and read that chart if you know what's best for you."

Panicked, Janet tries to think of something, anything, to say about the white blob the doctor is holding up, but it is no use. She can only stand there and cry.

"I remember feeling very confused, very frightened," she says. "I knew I had failed to do what they wanted me to do. And I knew that they were upset. What I now understand is that my father was afraid, my mom was afraid, and they were confused. Neither were high school graduates—they not only had to deal with the diagnosis, they had to understand it."

As it was, life in the United States had rarely seemed more incomprehensible and contradictory. It was 1968, a jittery year that saw cities explode in the wake of Martin Luther King's assassination, and the segregationist George Wallace make a third-party presidential bid. That year, seat belts became mandatory in new cars and the United States dropped more bombs on Vietnam than in all of World War II. Far from the turmoil, where the earth appeared a serene blue orb, the Apollo 8 astronauts were the first to look upon the dark side of the moon.

Playing out on a small, fuzzy TV screen, these seismic events were barely discernible to Janet, whose horizon contracted with a final diagnosis of retinitis pigmentosa. For some reason, the many doctors who came into the darkened exam rooms seemed fascinated as they peered at her dilated pupils. They talked animatedly among themselves and recommended that the remaining four of the Babbses' six children be examined for signs of RP.

"It's a rare disease," Janet says, "but even rarer in the African American community. Subsequently, four out of six of my siblings were diagnosed with it. The other two, one male and one female, are fully sighted and have no traces of the condition. I'm number two in the birth order. My older sister is not only blind but deaf as well."

With the Babbses' three daughters and a son in varying stages of vision loss, doctors mapping the disease progression found the situation was even more mystifying. Janet explains, "For most people, RP presents as losing your peripheral field, the side vision. Our form of RP is even rarer. Ours is backward. It starts with your central acuity, the vision you use to see distance, and it goes outward. Typically, in this form you can be losing central as well as peripheral vision. That's one of the reasons it was even rarer—and why we were such a topic of interest to the vision community."

For a child, it was a lot to process. "I can remember the day I received the diagnosis. And I went home that night after this long car trip from Boston. We had bunk beds, and I remember lying on the bed thinking, 'What is this thing they just told me that I have—that I can't even say? I'm not going to go to sleep until I can say the word: *retinitis pigmentosa*.' It was hard to put the two words together, then try to dissect it and digest it in terms of what it actually meant for me. I was very confused, worrying about silly stuff like, well—can I spell it? You start wondering: 'Wow—how different am I from other people? How am I going to go to school tomorrow and tell people I have this condition that I can't say or spell?' It's a long adjustment process."

If the Babbs children were minor celebrities at Massachusetts Eye and Ear, they stumbled toward the bottom of the pecking order on the playgrounds of Pittsfield. "We always had the little neighborhood skirmishes as kids do. If someone teased you and called you a blind bat, our reaction was you don't sit there, you go after them." Janet laughs at the memory of all that flailing and slapstick self-defense.

"There were fights and we would defend ourselves. Those same kids would bully other people, too—anyone different, whether it be your race, your ethnicity, it really didn't matter. Sooner or later you come to the realization that you can't go on beating up the world, that there's going to be somebody bigger and badder than you are. You learn to use your brain and have a sense of confidence that you can rise above that."

Running away on the playground was hardly an option as the vision loss progressed. And in a sorely taxed urban school system in the late sixties, adaptive equipment and in-school disability instructors were all but unheard of. "It was decided that we could not be educated in a public school system during that time. This is just at the beginning stages of special education. We really were not being offered an adequate education at home and we needed to go to a school that specialized in educating individuals who were blind."

Hey—why are they letting all those kids walk into the walls? Isn't this a school to help blind kids? Janet flinches at the thuds and groping hands. It's so cruel. Isn't it?

At twelve, she still has some usable sight, and she is appalled and frightened at the pratfalls and collisions that punctuate the beginning of the fall term at Perkins School for the Blind in Watertown, outside Boston. Finding one's way is just part of the orientation process, but she is feeling as though she's fallen into some strange, if welcoming, rabbit hole. She hardly speaks, but her thoughts are in turmoil: "I'm not blind all the way. What am I doing here? Where is Watertown? There's nobody here who looks like me. Who will help me braid my hair and match my clothes?"

Still, what astonishing luxuries there are for the Babbs children to discover: There are twenty or so students to a dorm cottage, with house parents, a cook, and maids. At home there were so many chores—dishes, laundry, bed making. Fantastic, Janet is thinking as the dinner plates are whisked off for someone else to scrub. Have I died and gone to heaven?

Soon enough, she learned that Perkins was no country club. "I didn't understand the demands that were going to be placed on me and the responsibility that I had to take on even as a twelve-year-old. Getting up and getting your clothes prepared for school, making sure that your hair looked okay and that you could shower and ID the proper clothing. I could do the hair braiding by touch, but one of the maids was African American and she would help me with my hair. I just didn't have enough vision to really make sure that I looked okay. It was very important, especially at that age."

Academics were rigorous, but for the first time since her vision loss, Janet was doing well in school. Learning Braille was mandatory, and the library was wondrously full of accessible volumes of history, fiction, and science. Chapel and classes began at 7:30 and ended at 4:30. After dinner, there was study time from seven to ten. It was a highly structured way of life. But Perkins offered another, unexpected freedom that Janet had thought was lost to her forever.

My, can this girl run. She was always fast before RP. And the coaches of Perkins's well-respected track-and-field team like what they have seen in Janet and her brother. The Babbses cannot afford to send money for sneakers, so the children are taken to a store in nearby Newton and fitted with their first Nikes at the school's expense.

Janet laces them up and cares for them proudly. She bounces to practice smiling and eager. And soon she is flying along the track, her finger slipped into a metal ring that runs along a guide wire to keep blind runners in their own lanes for the fifty- and hundred-yard dashes.

Zzzzzzz. The wire's hiss is her own sound barrier, and she means to push it. Her braids bounce in the wind she can feel again after being cautious and still for so very long. Coaches and students are hollering on the sidelines. She reaches deeper, runs faster. And in the shower, she is thrilled to feel hard, smooth muscle in her legs.

Janet wants more. And she wants to run harder. She settles on the 440, training hours a day until her body senses the slant and curves of the oval track, the precise width of a lane; her hearing is attuned to the close, hard breaths and footfalls of her competitors, just inches away. The impulse is strong: pull away, get out of traffic. Faster is safer. And it feels so very fine.

Janet wins, often—against blind and sighted high school runners. Crossing a finish line, there is nothing tentative about her.

"Our school won many, many events," she recalls. "My brother and I both broke national records. It was something we would never have known that we were good at. For me it was the four-forty, the fifty-yard dash, and the softball throw. My brother's events were the mile, the single broad jump, and the fifty-, seventy-five-, and hundred-yard dashes. And he was also on the wrestling team."

So why, at the end of her junior year, did she choose to abandon this supportive, trusting environment? "I decided that I really wanted to be able to go back to public school. It was important to me at that time. I really wanted to graduate high school with my peers back in Pittsfield. I went to my counselor and said, 'I think I want to go back home.'"

Everyone was against it, she says. No one left specialized schools to return to ill-equipped public schools then; the movement was all in the opposite direction. But Janet had an overriding concern. "My parents were getting divorced—there was a lot of turmoil in the family. And I think that I felt that I'd always been the family counselor. For me it was a very natural role to take on. I thought that by going back to school in Pittsfield I could have some sense of what was going on within the family. I knew it wasn't good. I was more worried being away."

Hindsight told her that it was a senseless sacrifice. "When I went back into high school, I went right back into the isolation. I was still the only blind person in the school. And I couldn't fix the family problems. It was not a good year for me."

She graduated with the help of an advocate she credits for much of her success today. Grace Johnson was known as an "itinerant teacher" then, a roving expert within the school system who oversaw students with visual impairments. "She was my savior," Janet says. "She would always check in on me, always be there after school if I needed the support academically. More important, I think she helped me reach a level of maturity that I really needed. She would say to me, 'You know, as bad as your family problems are, at some point you're going to have to make the decision to step out of it because you have to save yourself. I always had a sense of just being overly responsible—for the marriage, the siblings, whatever was going on. I think she helped me look at that reality."

It was a harsh but essential lesson: a life of advocacy can't begin until you can find the strength to take care of yourself. And that truth was underscored when Janet was a struggling college student. A freshman year at Fitchburg State College was disastrous, she says, in large part because she was too timid or uninformed to pursue the Braille texts and extra help she needed.

"I failed miserably. I didn't have a supportive family situation. I knew nobody. The only thing I knew was that I wanted to get as far away from Pittsfield as I could, and I had a small scholarship. Fitchburg had a program in special ed and I knew that I wanted to work with people who are blind. I wanted to be like Grace Johnson. I knew if I had a job like that I could do it."

The college disaster was a setback, but a series of low-skilled jobs got her motivated anew. "I worked in the parks division for part of a summer, then at a hospital in the kitchen, making salads. And that's when I knew I had to go to college." And she did, with more success. She would earn a BA from the University of Massachusetts in Boston, and an MA in education from Springfield College, where she met Russell. Along the way, she grew bolder and more resourceful as a student with special needs. Since she had been declared legally blind, she was an MCB client and well versed in getting the help that she needed—or so she thought until she hit a fateful stumbling block.

"As a result of my eye condition, I was having a lot of severe headaches. Sunlight was very detrimental to the progression of the eye disease, and being out with unprotected lenses was bad. During that time, Corning came out with these new glasses called CPF lenses for people who had difficulty with transitioning between indoors and bright sunlight. They were the first lenses that really filtered out the UV rays and gave you a sharper image. So when I first heard about them, I was very excited. I wanted to get these lenses."

Now known as GlareControl lenses, the Corning glasses with orange-brown tints could offer individuals with diabetic retinopathy and RP better visual function and reduced glare. The doctor Janet saw at New England College of Optometry in Boston told her that they had some CPF lenses she could try. At his direction, she looked out the window without them first, then through the lenses.

"It was incredible," she recalls. "The images were sharper—it was like filtering out a haze. So of course I got very excited about the glasses. He said they were three hundred dollars. I told him that three hundred dollars was the same as a million to me— I just didn't have it. He was confident the Commission for the Blind would help me pay for them."

"You can't have them."

Janet's counselor at the commission is unequivocal.

"But why not?"

"They're new and we don't know anything about them. And we won't pay for them."

Janet feels the first stirrings of activism beneath her anger and frustration.

"Who can I talk to? Do you have a supervisor? I want a chance for somebody to understand what these glasses mean to me."

"Put it in writing."

She does, and the supervisor says no. But Janet will not go away.

"Okay, what's the next step?"

"That was the next step."

Curiouser and curiouser, this bureaucratic catch-22. Pressing further, Janet is told that she can ask for an administrative hearing with the assistant commissioner, her counselor, a supervisor, and the commissioner.

"Okay, I'd like to appeal your decision."

Janet gets a hearing date and obtains a letter from the doctor who let her try the glasses, providing full clinical information on the lens innovations, a prescription, and an explanation of how the glasses could help her. She is terrified in the room full of upper-echelon MCB staffers, but she presents her case. A woman asks her a few questions and then delivers the verdict.

"No."

"Who are you?"

"I'm the assistant commissioner."

"Did you look at all the backup information I mailed you?"

"No."

"Is there an eye doctor on staff?"

"No."

"How do you make a decision when nobody here has looked at my chart, and nobody bothered to do any research? And you're just going to say no?"

"Yes."

Janet's anxiety has melted away in this absurdist kangaroo court. She is angry, but polite and controlled.

"Then I want to go above the Commission for the Blind, and I will take it as far as I need to. Because you can't tell me that you know who I am—that you know how I see and you know what would benefit me. Not without someone to help make a clinical decision."

The tribunal takes a short recess, and when they return, Janet is told she may have the glasses. She is thrilled, but she is not through. No other disabled people should have to push themselves through such an ordeal. She asks that the review policy within the agency be revised and considered on an individual basis—with a qualified clinical presence.

Yes, they say.

Janet is exhausted as she collects her documentation and leaves the hearing room. Tapping down the corridor with her cane, she is aware of someone following her. The woman catches up and addresses the persistent young petitioner.

"Do you have a job?"

"No."

"Would you like a job?"

"Doing what?"

"Client advocacy. It's what you just did. And I want you to come to work here."

"I still consider myself a client advocate," Janet says. "It was the foundation to go on to other jobs that I did within the commission." As she moved through various positions, she delivered services to clients and used mass transit with effective cane mobility. But the highly capable career woman who applied for a Fidelco guide dog in 1991 will admit to a condition that complicated the process at first: too much confidence. Like many people who still retain some usable vision, she was initially unable and unwilling to let a four-legged creature override her perceptions.

"The one thing I learned from having Xippy is that it's very difficult to hand over that trust to an animal. It's more difficult when you have a good amount of usable vision. That was probably the most difficult transition for me, going from using a cane to a dog. You're saying to the dog, 'Go ahead, I trust your judgment, and I'm just going to go with you.'"

And then you don't. Instructors are alert for a person looking around, unconsciously trying to second-guess the dog. With Xippy, Janet says, "I had enough usable vision. But I didn't have enough vision to see details that a dog would see. Because I have very diminished central vision and depth perception issues, I might misjudge something. If I was approaching a staircase, for example, I might know it's a staircase, but when you have depth problems you can be up at the top of that staircase and it looks almost like a ramp. There's no definition, you can't tell how many stairs there are, or whether there's a barrier in the middle."

Intellectually, she knew such misperception was one of the

main reasons she decided to get a dog. But try as she might, she could not manage the surrender. "It's still very difficult. You need to be able to say, 'All right, this isn't my responsibility right now, it's his.' You need to trust him enough to let him lead. You give the command, then you have to let go of that."

The reservations she had with Xippy were not a problem with Osbourne. Her vision had grown worse, and they had a very complicated job to do together. "The first trip I made was to a conference in San Diego. I stipulated in the beginning with Fidelco that I needed a dog that could tolerate being in a lot of meetings that can go four hours, that the dog could be quiet. It had to be really relaxed. I was in a place with Osbourne the other day where there was a huge, moving crowd in a hotel ballroom and corridor. He had to be able to navigate a thousand people. Then when we were seated he had to adjust."

And he could not have stage fright. "I give a lot of presentations, so if I go up to a podium, he has to be able to go up to that podium and be relaxed enough, once I get him settled, to be able to tolerate listening to me give boring speeches." She laughs, and says that if Fidelco hadn't come up with Osbourne at the time, she would gladly have waited for a dog that could meet her complex set of needs. He has been up to the task all along—even when Madam Commissioner took a most undignified pratfall in full public view.

"We were flying to San Diego from Hartford. It was rainy and sleety at the same time, hitting the airport's sliding glass doors. Apparently the paint they use gets very slippery when it rains. I took a step up and it was like being on a sheet of glass. Down I went. Osbourne was very excited and confused. When some of the airport personnel saw that I fell, they started coming toward me very rapidly. Osbourne got a little bit protective.

He put his body right in front of me and you could tell he didn't want them to come near me. I had to tell him it was okay, and I asked him to sit. He calmed down." Assessing the damage, she found nothing was broken "except my pride."

Theirs is a very tight bond now, she says—but with ample room for Russell. "My husband is a huge dog fan—he was looking forward to this as much as I was. We were both very excited when Osbourne arrived. He knows that I'm the primary person that this dog has to bond with, and so for the first month, I really did not encourage any additional interaction between him and the dog. I don't ever ask him to feed the dog: that needs to come from me. But at home when we take the dog out to play, they interact very well. If I'm out of the room, he'll play with Russ, but then he'll realize, *Oh, she's not here*, and he'll go searching for me."

Like so many guide dog users, she has been surprised at how attuned they are in terms of personality. "He has a very playful side, and I think that matches me. Even though I'm an administrator, I'm very people oriented. He loves people, loves to go different places. We're very comfortable with each other now: the bond is just incredible. I can read his personality and know areas that he's going to have difficulty with. I know that if we go to a brand-new place, he's going to surge a little more. And he'll have a tendency to pull in new places. He's a little bit anxious sometimes. So I know to talk to him, be a little more verbal, a little more consoling with him in new places. If I'm in a hotel, I'll walk around the hotel with him, go back and forth to my room a couple of times so that he gets the message that we're going to be here, this is the home we're going to be staying in. And I ask him to find the room. So I'm constantly working him."

Outside, the afternoon is darkening and the storm has not let up. Osbourne has wandered over from his spot behind Janet's desk for his regular look-see; he does not care to let her out of his sight, and performs an antic, glad-to-see-ya dance even after a five-minute absence for a trip to the ladies' room. She strokes the big head nudging her, tells him he is a good dog, a wonderful guy. Sleet and snow are audibly pinging at the office windows as she asks, "Time to sharpen our skills on ice, Oz?"

Tony has arrived with a sheaf of messages. Phones shrill from the outer office. Duty calls the commissioner, and with a glance toward the snowy window, Osbourne beats a hasty retreat behind the desk.

"Smart boy," she says, smiling. "Such a very smart dog."

CHAPTER SIX

JUST LUCKY, I GUESS

Upton walked me around a rattlesnake once. I could hear it rattling on the other side of him. He got me right out of the area. And I'm going, "Good dog, good dog! Let's get you a treat."

—David Bearden

A greenish glare and the distant rumble of thunder greet a traveler to Hernando County, a scrubby, semi-rural tract of west central Florida patchworked with citrus groves, convenience stores, and migrant housing. Along Cortez Boulevard, a fast, gravel-spitting four-lane highway, scattered neighborhoods of one-story homes are landscaped with well-husbanded areca palms and hibiscus, wrecked Pontiacs or creative ways with chain link—depending on the homeowners' notion of outback feng shui. The largest employer here in Brooksville is Wal-Mart's mammoth "truck-to-truck" distribution center, 1.6

million square feet of disposable diapers, frozen cod fillets, shot-guns, and chain saws.

Pull off Cortez, navigate into the dusty residential neighborhood prosaically called Hill 'n Dale, and the slam of a car door sets off the throaty rumble of pit bulls, hunting beagles, and Rottweilers straining against a rattling kennel fence in a nearby yard.

"Welcome," says David Bearden, "to our little bit of heaven." He is smiling as he holds open the front door a robber once walked through in broad daylight—right past David, who was in the front yard watering his flowers and unable to see him. The man helped himself to David's wallet and watch atop a bedroom dresser, then sauntered back and knocked his victim over on his way out.

A low, nonaggressive "ruff" greets a stranger from within the small, tidy house. It comes from Upton, David's guide dog. Things have been well-monitored and secure around here, he says, since the arrival of the dogs. "Everything is better because of the dogs. Everything." Upton is his second Fidelco shepherd, he begins explaining. He replaced Isaac, who was attacked by unleashed dogs seventeen times and had to be retired.

"But I'm getting ahead of myself," David says, grinning. "Let's take one disaster at a time."

Al Capp, creator of that corn-fed lug Li'l Abner, also dreamed up a Dogpatch denizen he dubbed Joe Btfsplk, a guy with an unpronounceable name, an abundantly kind heart, and a mother lode of contagious bad karma. Capp drew him with a sunny smile and a perpetual black cloud over his head.

Joe Btfsplk has nothing on David Bearden, a wry, indomitable sort who is a mighty magnet for bad luck—draws it to himself like knives to a butcher block. Thus far, he has survived the aforementioned rattlesnake, a marauding pit bull, fires, robbery, mugging, and a passel of bibulous neighbors who think it's sporting to shoot bottle rockets at the blind guy's house. Not that all the trouble comes from without; since he suffered sudden, cataclysmic vision loss in 1989, David has burned up his kitchen stove five times that he can remember in his relentless pursuit of self-sufficiency.

"So sue me, I like to cook," he says, tucking his shoulder-length gray hair into a ponytail against the humidity. "And with all these kids, I have no choice."

Ah yes, the children. David has been a single parent of three daughters almost as long as he has been blind. Somehow, he is still smiling through it all, and doing his best to remain what Fidelco trainers call a "high user" of his guide dog. With no transportation—some taxicabs out here have consistently, if illegally, refused to service him with a dog—he and Upton regularly walk the two-mile round trip beside whizzing traffic on Cortez Boulevard to buy food and supplies at an outlying convenience store. They also travel the state by bus as activists for disability rights, and to promote guide dog awareness. Upton is usually in the wings when David performs as a lounge singer—generally for charity events—with prerecorded backup music and some wicked impersonations. For local club gigs, he makes just enough, he says, "to pay for a sitter and a taxi." But back in the day, he notes, "I opened for the Village People when they played Florida. And Eartha Kitt."

He came to his current and chief vocation when his three daughters were about to fly the nest. "I am the first single, legally blind foster parent in the United States," he says—adding that at least no one in the child welfare system has heard of another. As the unequivocal first blind foster parent in the state of Florida, David gives local children respite from the shambles of homelessness, crime, poverty, abuse, and abandonment. They are almost all in need of some form of therapy: preteens who were born crack babies and are now struggling with learning disabilities, damaged survivors of fetal alcohol syndrome, bereft orphans, and victims of emotional, physical, and sexual abuse. They are Asian, Latino, Caucasian, African American. They arrive on his doorstep with social workers, minimal luggage, and heartbreaking histories.

"One was openly gay and the parents just couldn't handle it," David offers by way of example. "So I ended up with him. Another kid was developmentally delayed. His mother couldn't handle the fact that he was mentally retarded and she kept dropping him off at the shelter every two weeks. He'd go home for a day, then she'd take him back there."

Licensed by the state in 2006, David feeds and shelters the foster children; supervises their therapy, medication, and homework; confers with their teachers; and celebrates their birthdays. They stay for days, weeks, or months, depending on their pending placements. There are always so many issues with each young wayfarer that the county-appointed therapist makes house calls. Only one boy has had to be removed as unmanageable. He tore the front door off its hinges—but he backed off when Upton expressed his loud disapproval. At last count, fifty-eight boys have found refuge in this snug, well-cared-for home filled with flea market treasures, family artwork, and carefully stowed footwear.

"There are tons of sneakers here—which can just lay me out flat if I trip over them."

At the moment, there are four boys living here: "I have my

adopted son Malcolm, who's visually impaired. He was shot in the eye with a slingshot when he was three, and he has no depth perception on the other side. He's fifteen. And I have Chad, who's eleven. I'm in the process of adopting him, and his two brothers, who will come soon. Then I have Rick [not his real name], who's going to be eighteen in a couple of days. He's getting ready to age out of the foster system and he's going to be moving in with a friend's family, because he's still got another year of high school left."

Rick, who has just gone to his room whooping over some birthday cookies David bought him, has been somewhat of a challenge to maintain on the $16.50-a-day stipend allotted for each foster child. He is at least six-four and can inhale half a chicken and a sack of burgers as a light snack. A fourth boy is recovering from horrific abuse and injuries. Traumatized and wary when he arrived, he was able to come tentatively out of his shell by talking about a safe, neutral subject: the dog. And Upton has helped with rehab; they have walked miles together, the three of them, to rebuild strength and muscles—and talk.

Over this long, sultry day, as children of all ages flow in and out, David details the events that took his sight, and the subsequent hard-knock odyssey that has made him a tireless—and some might say relentless—activist for disability rights. He campaigns for everything from improved standardized school testing for the visually impaired to stronger penalties for those who harm and incapacitate service dogs.

Narrating his extraordinary story, his tone is alternately matter-of-fact and mad-as-heck, but never self-pitying. He has no time for that. And besides, he insists, he is one extremely grateful man. He is sure that Isaac and Upton have both saved his life more than once, kept him sane, improved his family's lives, and propelled him through a series of escapades he would never have dreamed of. "Upton and I went skiing in Colorado," he says. "And I can't wait to go again."

Upton is not a movie poster shepherd. He is lean and dun-colored, of medium build. David, who is legally blind with just 20 percent vision in one eye and none in the other, finds him gorgeous: "Upton is trim, but we walk a lot. In the wintertime, when his coat is thick, he's really red—very pretty. He's a beautiful dog. And I love him. He's sweet."

Upton is also a stable, fiercely conscientious service animal. During her long career as a breeder, Robbie Kaman has found that the pretty boys—those bright-eyed, perfect confirmation pups—are not necessarily the finest working dogs. As she explained to a conference of fellow shepherd breeders, "It is not unusual to see a top working dog that to the observer is apt to be unimpressive, lacking in substance, maybe a bit light in the eye, under-angulated, short in neck, croup, body, or ears, drab in the pigment. . . . The mind, on the other hand, is able and willing to perform tasks under very stressful conditions with a bright, quick mental attitude and aptitude."

"Fire!" somebody is yelling. "We're on fire!"

The bus bringing David, Upton, and their fellow disability-rights advocates back from a day's lobbying at the state capital in Tallahassee has pulled over to the side of a busy road; smoke billows from the motor in the rear. The flames have gone out, but the interior is filling with smoke, and all the other passengers are able to file off quickly.

"What's happening? What?"

Seated way in back, David can feel his chest begin to tighten as the acrid chemical fumes trigger an asthma attack; he can sense a growing darkness overhead.

He is too overcome to shout a command to the dog, but it's not necessary. Upton is on his feet and tugging even before David begins to wheeze. They are moving into the aisle and forward; Upton's head is below the smoke and he is looking up at the distressed man, then at the aisle ahead, taking them forward quickly and deliberately—but smoothly, without a trace of panic, and not too fast for David, who is now trying to inhale in ragged gasps.

Suddenly, David can feel a breeze on his face. Upton has stopped to signal a step down, then a second. David is barely aware of his surroundings as the dog guides him away from the bus, around some hedges, and up over a parking lot. Upton is making his own judgments about finding a safe haven from the toxic cloud and ongoing traffic as David gags, unable even to hear properly in the chaos.

"Sir, you need help?"

The dog has brought him to that familiar haven— a gas station/convenience store. David's knees buckle with exhaustion and relief. His hands on the animal's body tell Upton what he is too overcome to speak.

Good dog. Heck of a dog. My hero.

"It was unbelievable," David says of that incident, which happened just a few days ago. "Upton didn't run, he didn't jerk." He is amazed that the shepherd exhibited no instinct to bolt— a reaction that would be natural to any animal in that situation. The dog was fine after the experience, but David is still struggling with the aftereffects. He keeps an inhaler within reach on the coffee table, as well as his ever-present can of Diet Coke to slake a dry, raspy throat. After a sip, he notes that his valorous shepherds have been equally proficient with life's more mundane tasks: "Both my dogs have been trained to find Diet Coke. I don't like Pepsi. I could train them to find the Diet Coke bottle because it's silver."

He says he taught his daughters to recognize and retrieve the fizzy stuff when they acted as his shopping guides before the dogs came. And "find the Diet Coke" was a wildly popular part of the guide dog awareness programs David and his first dog, Isaac, did in local public schools. "We'd take Isaac and the different soda cans into the schools and let the kids hide them—but in plain sight." The elementary students were attentive when David explained a guide dog's other wonders—leading him safely along and across busy roads, helping him onto taxis and buses and in stores. They stayed engaged when he explained guide dog etiquette—how a working dog should not be petted, fed, or played with. But the Diet Coke trick drew shrieks of amazement and delight every time. Isaac never missed.

"He was such a smart dog."

David says he is equally amazed by Upton, though he still exhibits some boisterous puppy behavior when he is out of harness. He has jumped on the bed and pilfered food, and he likes to run exuberantly around the house. Not long ago, Upton gently but persistently herded a group of David's daughters and their friends in the backyard onto the small porch until they hollered, "Dad, make him stop."

"He's like any teenager," says David, who corrects the dog when need be, and does not care to imagine life without him. Though he is ever watchful of the front door and investigates all comers, Upton seems unfazed by the ebb and flow in this bursting-at-the-seams bungalow. Some of the personnel: Maggie, Malcolm's cuddly, hyperkinetic chihuahua/border collie mix; the changing roster of foster children and their therapists; David's grown daughters Cristyn, Brittany, and Marissa and their babies; plus social workers, state inspectors, and disability activists.

Sometimes Upton himself is part of the ongoing therapy in this house. "If Malcolm is stressed, I'll ask him to help me wash the dog or brush him. It's very calming. The foster kids talk about the dogs they had at their houses. And we'll walk with him a lot." Outings with Upton can be more informative than the cursory case file provided with an arriving child. "I make the new kid walk with me all the time because I usually walk two miles a day with Upton. In that time, they open up. So if you've got a good idea of what their history is and what to look for systematically, in most cases they'll tell you."

He considers Upton a full partner in his work with the children. "The dog has not only given me my freedom. He's helped to educate and settle the foster children that I have." He is also a gentle enforcer. Just imagine what an arriving foster child—who most often has good reasons to distrust adults—might try to pull on a foster dad who can't see. But Upton schools them quickly.

Lesson one: all disobedient strays will be summarily herded. "Upton is fast," David says. "He instantly learns the name of every foster kid who comes into the house. We'd introduce the kids to the dog and he'd know their name and know their smell. They would try to take off in a store and hide and I'd just tell him to go find them. And he will go locate the kid I tell him to find." Recently, when one boy went to play at a place in the neighborhood that had been declared out of bounds, David set Upton on the trail. When they found him, the truant's jaw dropped as he muttered, "Busted by a dog." David laughs at the boy's wonderment all the way home. "They all go, 'How does he do it? How does he know where I'm at?' I say, 'Well, that's his job.'"

David has observed that despite his herding talents, Upton can be of most help to troubled children in a very passive mode. "What I find is that most kids who have disorders and disabilities, especially kids who have problems in learning, just gravitate toward him. They'll sit down and pet the dog and we'll talk about things they're having problems with. They're just petting the dog and talking. They don't know what to do with it all, what's been happening to them. We'll get books that they can read, or talking books. They'll try to read the book while they're listening to it on tape, and they'll sit there with the dog the whole time." Children who have suffered physical or emotional injury may respond to Upton when they are unable to talk about their painful recent pasts. "One of the kids had post-traumatic stress syndrome super bad. When he got really scared and nervous, he'd ask if he could pet the dog. The dog turns out to be doing double duty, doing therapy."

Thus, since he arrived the day after New Year's Day 2008, Upton continues to evolve and expand his roles as a service dog. At night, he also functions as David's ears, since he uses a machine to control his sleep apnea and might not hear a boy trying to slip out of the house. "They know from day one that nothing gets past Upton. He'll alert me the second anyone goes near the door." Upton also respects special dispensations. One highly anxious boy was allowed to step outside and pace in the driveway at night until he was calm enough to sleep. Upton waited up, and saw him safely inside.

John Byfield, who lives an hour east of David and has trained him with both of his guide dogs, knew exactly what kind of replacement to request when Isaac was retired. "David is an active person. We needed a dog that was active, so that David would not be restricted. We needed a dog that's adaptable, since David works at schools, takes courses, and is in state office buildings doing legislative lobbying and the like. We needed a dog that could switch it on and off. Because of the problems with Isaac and the aggressive dogs in the neighborhood, we also needed a dog that was not confrontational with other dogs—that would not look for trouble. I told the staff at Fidelco all of this and they came up with Upton—absolutely the right dog."

Both dogs, he agrees, had to contend with the demanding pace of a unique individual. "David is very involved with everything—that's his nature. He has a lot of ability and interests. There were always transportation difficulties for him, and his eyes have gotten progressively worse over the years. He just felt that he needed some help with traveling. It's a busy household, he always had foster kids, and some of them require careful handling. David is very fair, but he's a disciplinarian. He doesn't stand any nonsense."

Years of adversity have left David with a workable ratio of self-discipline and easy humor—often at his own expense. With evident pride, he will tell you that he made the neat, crisply bordered drapes himself—then point out the one panel that has its banana leaf pattern stitched in upside down. "You didn't notice? Good. Maybe I can't thread the needle, but I can run a good straight seam."

David is matter-of-fact about his domestic accomplishments and privations. But he is adamant on one essential point: to appreciate the true value of his Fidelco shepherds, you must have some understanding of what life was like without them. He has been legally blind for twenty years now. The first fourteen, "the predog era," were fraught with the kind of struggle and pathos that draws construction and film crews to the aid of beleaguered families on *Extreme Makeover: Home Edition*.

"The dogs are my makeover miracles," he says. "For all of us—me, my daughters, all these foster kids. It's no exaggeration to say that they gave me a purpose in life beyond mere survival. They're just so smart, and so willing to work. In a way, they make you live up to their standards."

David was born in Dallas fifty-two years ago, to a Mexican mother and a white father whose outraged parents eventually induced him to abandon his young biracial family—leave them sitting, homeless, on a curb—when David was four. "I'd experienced discrimination in Texas because my mom is Mexican and my dad is white," he recalls. "Back then in the sixties, we didn't have any rights." Things were not much better in Florida, where his mother, Marguerita Roma, moved her three children. Life was still hard, and David says that her schooling in the basics saved him when he lost his sight.

"Having grown up in Texas before the Depression and being poor, my mom taught me all the skills I need for survival. I learned how to make do with what you had. I can wash clothes on a scrub board, hang them on the line, and iron them. She taught me how to make bread, how to bake. I used to spend my summers doing alterations with my grandmother. She had a dry cleaner's in Lakeland. She taught me how to sew. We grew up making clothes."

Marguerita also taught her children the rudiments of social

advocacy. In 1982, she founded and still directs Farmworkers Self-Help, a migrant worker empowerment program in the Dade City area. Serving the 15,000 farmworkers living in adjoining Pasco County and environs, the nonprofit provides emergency food and clothing, medical and dental care, housing help, and advocacy on issues from health problems to exploitative labor practices. David notes that visual impairment is common when agricultural workers in dusty fields rub their eyes after working with pesticide-treated crops.

He and all his children pitch in with volunteer work. In 2005, when hurricane-damaged citrus crops made for an especially meager Christmas in migrant worker families, the *St. Petersburg Times* dropped in as David led his daughters, a nephew, and a few other children through a weeklong cookie baking marathon to add just a little sweetness—fifty batches' worth—to two hundred nearly barren tables. A few of the young bakers had disabilities, from learning problems to osteogenesis imperfecta (soft bones). They burned a few cookies and blew out a fifteen-year-old mixer, but they got the job done—with a quiet, unspoken bonus, according to Rose Rocco, chairwoman of the local chapter of the National Federation for the Blind, who was on hand to help. She told the *St. Petersburg Times* reporter: "All of these kids, even though they have a disability, they are all achievers and one thing David wants to show them is they can do many things themselves."

David deadpanned: "We always have a fire extinguisher."

"Upton, quit that!"

Upton is scratching—the insects and heat can be a torment to a large, hairy dog here, and David must see to regular flea dips and grooming. He bathes the dog and keeps him as cool as possible, saving long walks for evenings during the worst of the summer heat, so that the pavement does not blister Upton's paws. The dog stops mid-scratch, circles twice, and settles down for a snooze as the darker part of David's tale unfolds.

In 1989, he was married and starting a new job. The youngest of the girls was eight months old when a freak accident over the December holidays changed everything. David recalls, "I was working in a hospital in Florida. I went in at an entry-level position so I could get my training in the lab. And three days after I got my license to do phlebotomy—blood drawing—I was doing labs in the ICU."

The hospital is understaffed three days after Christmas as David leaves the ICU to discard sharps—needles, broken test tubes—in the designated area. When he arrives there, the sharps boxes are overflowing, and no one has emptied any of the containers or taken out the bagged waste. Newly licensed and eager to follow compliance standards, David grabs a bulging biohazard bag to take it to the disposal site.

It happens in a second; he does not notice that sharps have been improperly bagged with biohazard waste that generates gases. As he lifts the bag, a sharp object punctures the plastic and the expanding gases blow the contents straight into David's face. He staggers to the ER, where no physician is available. David flushes his eyes out himself and fills out the report with the help of the head nurse. Despite the fact that he has multiple lacerations from potentially infectious sharps and debris, he is released without further treatment—and without a course of preventative antibiotics.

Within three days, a raging staph infection has destroyed his corneas. He is also diagnosed with neuro meningitis and suffers a stroke.

When he awakens, he cannot see.

"I was totally blind in the beginning," he says. "Then I got twenty-six percent vision back in my right eye, but nothing in the left. Just lucky, I guess."

He says the hospital has since shut down, owing to the fallout from his accident, and numerous other persistent health and safety violations. "So I'm home, I'm blind—with three daughters. A three-year-old, a two-year-old, and an eight-month-old. And as soon as I got the cane, their mom walked out the door."

His wife left for good—without the children. Enter the child welfare authorities. "The hospital reported me to the Department of Children and Families, because I had these three children and they didn't think a blind person would be capable of caring for kids. Obviously, it was very difficult the first couple months. But I kept on the phone with Lighthouse for the Blind."

He had endless questions for their experts. How do I mix formula? Do laundry? How do I know what's in the cabinets?

"They talked me through everything on the phone. I got some people from a church who came and helped me. It was tough going. I had to prove to them I could do it. They gave me two weeks before the home inspection. My house was immaculate, everything was in its place, the cabinets were done. I didn't have any Braille skills, but I knew what I was buying. Everything was organized so that there were no mistakes."

The key to survival was in the details. "With the formula, I had the scoop to measure the correct amount. I got bottles that only had the right volume. I got a feeder bottle for baby food. I didn't have to worry about a spoon—I wasn't good at that at all. It was just very difficult to have two other children at the time." To keep tabs on the two walkers, he did what some busy sighted parents resort to: "I put bells on their shoes, and they were forbidden to take the bells off. That way I could hear where they were. I did learn how to safety-pin all their outfits together, I had a big diaper pin on the back of everybody's dress." As they grew, he taught his girls to pin and cut pattern pieces, and he made some of their clothes. Since he couldn't afford a washing machine, he used a scrub board and tub in the backyard.

All of it—the neat, organized home that would pass routine inspections, the constant vigilance—would later help him pass muster in maintaining a safe, licensed, and well-run foster home. Years of hypervigilance with his own children have attuned him to the slightest sound or whiff of trouble. "None of the kids can get away with anything. I know every sound. My son went in the kitchen—he was snitching cookies—and I hear the bag rattle and yell, 'Get out of those cookies.'"

Despite his organizational and domestic skills, life in the boonies without transportation was difficult indeed. Cristyn, the youngest daughter, has been beset with a variety of ailments, from apnea to rheumatoid arthritis to fibromyalgia. As an infant, she required constant monitoring; incessant medical visits were difficult to manage. Just getting to the store for bread and milk was a trial—and somewhat of a neighborhood spectacle.

Who or what is that staggering through the heat-glimmering streets of Hill 'n Dale on a sweltering morning? It has eight arms, eight legs, and a long hose.

Lord, it's that poor blind fella and his kids. Wife up and left, the authorities always after him to snatch those babies, and no supermarkets or drug stores way out here. Tch.

Cristyn, ten months old, is large for her age, plumped to thirty-three pounds by steroids and so unwell that she is on an apnea monitor day and night. So there she is, strapped to David's chest in a baby carrier with the hose hanging down, and Brittany, the two-year-old, is in another carrier strapped to his back. He is using a cane with his right hand, holding the hand of three-year-old Marissa with the left. Over his shoulder he has slung a diaper bag, and the clunky apnea monitor.

Sweat has sluiced down his back and chest before they've gone a block. To stay focused in the heat, David calculates his burden: he is hauling about a hundred pounds of babies and equipment. They may look crazy, but they are a family.

He pushes on, before the sun gets too high.

"I did it every day. I had to. I didn't have a choice."

There is still some anger in his voice as he recalls those grim days.

"My mother said, 'They're your kids, don't come crying to me. They're very young and you've got a long life ahead of you, so you'd better figure it out now. Because I'm not doing it—I raised my children. I understand you're blind. Get over it. You have two choices: you can crawl in a hole and die or get off your ass and do something about it.'"

He says he was furious at her. How dare she? Didn't she realize he was blind?

"Yeah," she shot back, "so what?"

The woman wouldn't lift a pot. "She helped me financially, but as far as cleaning and cooking and taking care of the children, nope. She made me have to do it. It was tough love. She was not going to let me crawl in a hole and die. Had she not done that, I probably would have sat in that chair and faced the wall for the rest of my life. Depression hits really hard, and it's tough to get past that. You just have to work through it day by day."

He concedes that her gruff stance was hard for him to accept at the time. But this is a woman whose life is spent advocating for the have-nots on even grimmer issues—such as the plight of a migrant worker's child run over by a tractor and denied medical treatment, resulting in her death. This is hardscrabble Florida, not camera-ready South Beach.

It was a long time before David received more than a token compensation for his disability. "When it first happened, I was on Workman's Comp. I got five hundred dollars a month for three kids. They were forcing me to do job searches—without any training. Then if they decided I hadn't done an adequate job search, they just wouldn't pay me for the month. I couldn't drive. I couldn't read the business section in the phone book to call people."

Not surprisingly, there were few jobs of any kind for an untrained blind person. "It was a tough couple of years. Fortunately, my mom was able to pull me through and help me to pay my bills. As soon as they said I was permanently blind, Workman's Compensation settled and they cut my check, which I bought this house with. I paid my mom back every penny."

He does not like to look back at his own anger during that time; he admits it was not a pretty picture. "It took me a long time to quit being pissed off about being blind. I was mad at everybody. I was not a nice person to be around. I don't know how my kids could stand me. Then one day a switch clicked on and I realized that I could advocate for myself. I just had to figure out how to do it without being angry. Once I got rid of the anger, I realized that I couldn't change it—the blindness was never going to go away. Now what am I going to do with the rest of my life?"

Raising the girls had kept that larger question at bay; he was just too busy to think about it. He says that to his surprise, the darkest point came about fifteen years after the accident. "It was when I knew my kids were going to be gone. My youngest daughter was sixteen, she'd be out of the house in two years, and I knew I was going to be alone with a cane in an area without public transportation. It was a very sad, low point. I had just twenty percent left in the one eye, and I'm probably going to lose that with normal aging. I'll get to where there's nothing but light perception. The prognosis is depressing. So am I going to be proactive about it, or am I going to let it cause me—really—to die? I'm not ready to crawl in a hole. I don't want to do that."

His cane skills were good, but with his guide babies growing up and out, he had to rethink his mobility and dependency issues.

"Why did I go for the dog? As they got older, my daughters were tired of dragging me around, quite frankly. They grew up most of their lives here, and I usually just had one of my kids and my cane to get around. I'd become reliant on the children, and they needed to be independent and free of me. So I went out looking for a guide dog school where I could get them to come to where I live."

A residential school was not an option. "There's no way. I had three kids in school, and none of my family could leave their jobs to care for them for a month. And I don't have a lot of friends that aren't visually impaired or blind. That's usually the group I socialize with."

Attending a regular current-events group at the Lighthouse for the Blind, he heard about Fidelco from a staffer who had just gotten an e-mail describing their In-Community Placement. "I called them," says David, "and met John Byfield. He came down and walked with me one day. They have to assess you. He was already here working with somebody else. It took almost two years before I got my first dog. At the time there weren't any dogs available."

Salvation arrived in mid-January of 2003. "John showed up one day with this big old sable German shepherd named Isaac. I knew I would no longer be trusting my children or my cane."

Nonetheless, that two-mile round trip to the store at the gas station, so numbingly familiar to him, took on new terrors. "I knew that I was going to have to trust this dog to get me there and back. I was scared to death. But the minute I got that harness on the dog and actually took off down the street, oh my gosh. I felt, 'I am so free. I can go as fast as I want.' I was always having to tell my kids to hurry up, speed up. Oh my God, it was so free."

They gelled quickly as a team. And they enjoyed a few months of giddy optimism, until new and terrifying challenges threatened their partnership—and turned David into a committed activist.

In July 2003, the *Hernando Times* ran a large portrait of Isaac on page one, with an account of a vicious attack he had suffered a month earlier. The story opened with David and Isaac standing at a busy Brooksville intersection in the pouring rain. David held up a soggy sign to passing motorists that read: "This isn't my Pet. He's my EYES. Protect Service Dogs. Florida Statute 413081."

He was protesting local authorities' lack of action on that unprovoked attack by a loose dog in his neighborhood. He and Isaac had been walking in the evening, on a familiar road that they had trained on. The reporter Duane Bourne described the attack:

> In a flash, he heard the rustle as the dog hit the cattle gate. Then, he heard a grating noise—the dog's paws scratching the ground outside the fence.
>
> "The next thing I know is that he had a hold of Isaac," Bearden recalled.
>
> Isaac had positioned himself between Bearden and the attacking dog, a Labrador mix twice his size. Soon, both were wailing. The noise caught the attention of motorist David Smith, who flashed his headlights and yelled to scare the dog away. Smith then summoned the authorities.
>
> "Isaac was just lying there," Bearden said.
>
> As a result of the attack, Isaac was bleeding from his stomach, his hind quarters and elbows—20 puncture wounds in all. The unvaccinated dog bit Bearden on his ankle and right ear. . . .
>
> Moments later, the owner, who was later identified in the county's dangerous dog complaint as Lucille Christman, perhaps hearing Bearden's cries for help, opened her door and called for her dog. When the dog didn't respond, she came outside, retrieved the

Labrador mix and slammed the door behind her, a report said.

Nearly 45 minutes later, a sheriff's deputy responded. An animal control officer was also called to the scene.

"This is not an animal control issue. This is a crime. I want this woman arrested," Bearden recalled saying.

Under state law, anyone who injures or kills or permits a dog they own to injure or kill a guide dog or service animal is guilty of a misdemeanor and must pay restitution.

Nothing happened. Supervisor of Animal Services James Varn declared that he knew of no such law. The state attorney's office dismissed the complaint and refused comment; a civilian review panel declared that the attacking dog was not dangerous. Following the publicity, a truckload of self-styled vigilantes drove up to the blind troublemaker's house and menaced him until Isaac loudly scared them off. Shortly after, when spooked by another loose dog, Isaac tried to run and was injured when a branch tore his paw.

Isaac was diminished, but David was galvanized. He told the reporter, "The only way they are going to get me to shut up is to shoot me. If I have to be the squeakiest little wheel, I will. I will stand outside the courthouse every day until I get justice."

And he was true to his word. The coffee table is piled with clippings from this new activist era, with headlines such as DENIED ENTRY, MAN SEEKS JUSTICE. That time it was a gas station owner who refused to let him enter and buy a soda with the dog. David had just spent a long afternoon walking the sidewalks in Brooksville to reinforce the dog's traffic skills on curbs and concrete. Isaac was in harness, with a tag John Byfield had given them citing Florida guide dog law. David says he explained the law three times before the man ordered them out, yelling that the dog would eat his food. Seeing the commotion, a nearby deli owner welcomed them and provided drinks, and the police were summoned.

By then, David was president of the National Federation for the Blind for Hernando and east Pasco counties. And he had learned a new, more effective mode of advocacy from Marion Gwizdala, president of the Florida Association of Guide Dog Users, who had overseen many such discrimination cases.

"Marion called me when he saw an article in the paper. We ended up having hundreds of people with guide dogs marching. The people at the association taught me how to lobby and advocate for myself and how to do it properly. Early on, I was just screaming and yelling. I was mad. I knew I was right, I knew they were wrong—but they weren't listening. And I didn't know how to make them listen. I've since learned how."

At this point, he can probably recite Florida Statute 413081 in his sleep. Spewing that legalese, he has found that formerly uninterested peace officers, county commissioners, and animal control personnel snap to attention as its crisp, unequivocal prescriptives spell out the violations and their penalties. "The secret is to know where to get the law, and have it verbatim. When you go to the meetings, you can give them each copies of it because they won't go to look it up themselves. They're just going to tell you, 'We'll have to put this under advisement.' But they can't put you off like that when you show them—here's the law, it's in black and white, here are the statutes, it's in your hand, you're going to comply or you're going to get sued. It's that simple. You'll either follow the law or I'll make you follow the law. I have rights and you're not going to take them away."

He grins, and admits he has befriended more than a few former adversaries. "Now they call me if there's an issue they need clarification on. It's changed a lot."

But David has not relaxed his vigilance. Things do still happen to guide dog users all over Florida. "We've all been thrown out of everything, restaurants, gas stations. Wal-Mart threw me out twice. And they won't do it again. After the second time, I called the deputy and I stood up there and I gave him the law. Oddly enough, there is a book that the deputies carry and it has all the Florida laws in it. But the guide dog laws are not in there."

Stranger still, he says, is the fact that animal control issues a large tag that has the access law on it. "It's right there on the harness—it's a great big brass tag. It's free. They give it to everybody with a service dog. And they weren't even complying with their own law."

The deputy summoned to Wal-Mart would not even look at the tag, David says. He and Isaac stayed put. "I said, 'Call your supervisor. And bring him down here now. I'm not going to move until you do. The deputy was mad, but he got his supervisor. It ended up being Sheriff Nugent. And he really started advocating for us."

Like Nina Bektic and Vicky Nolan, who brought civil complaints against discriminatory restaurants and cabdrivers, David says he would endure the trouble and discomfort of a lawsuit if it might make things easier for the many visually impaired people who are unable or unwilling to challenge discrimination. "There are times when we could have sued the county and won," he says. "It would have been horrible, but I was willing to do it."

Too often, he has observed, people who will not abide by reason or a recitation of the law will respond to the threat of a lawsuit. "I find that if you get them in their wallets, they'll listen. So you give them the law, you tell them, 'You must comply, and it's very clear what the consequences are if you don't.' A lot of the violations have monetary and jail-time penalties attached."

Winning the hearts and minds of the next generation of restaurateurs and gas station owners was a priority when David and Isaac began visiting local schools. They were enthusiastically received, and soon, they saw results. "I could go anywhere with Isaac, say in a store, and the kids would go, 'Look, there's Isaac. You can't touch him, he's working.' You'd hear the kids tell parents that. And now you hear parents telling their kids. For the last six years, we've been doing education in the county and it's paid off. It's horrible that all the difficulties cost me a great dog. The only thing that makes it worthwhile is that the education is immeasurable. There's no way that anyone could have afforded to put that kind of advertising out there—public service announcements or whatever. But we were in the media nonstop for five years. And it worked out."

But it was too late for Isaac. Loose dogs cannot be held at bay with statute books. The trouble continued—and grew more complex. "In one of the attacks, I dislocated my elbow and my knee. And EMS refused to transport me because I had a guide dog. They said somebody might be allergic. But they had to transport me with the dog. Unless they're using unusual precautions, or if there's blood involved. Or the dog is aggressive toward them.

That was their policy. We found the law, we looked it up, and they had to change their policy."

John Byfield, who had worked with David and Isaac after the initial attacks, says he did what he could in a highly inhospitable area. "We tried to get Isaac more comfortable with the dogs. But there were two or three other incidents. We just walk out in his neighborhood and unleashed dogs are all over the place. The plan was that the moment Isaac alerts to another dog, David had to talk to him and try to keep him moving away from the dog. Most loose dogs tend to be territorial. They protect the area of their house and their yard. If you can get past them, the probability is that they won't pursue you. That was something we worked on and had some success with. He learned where the dogs were. David called animal control, but they were not responsive initially. So you try to avoid the area where you had an encounter. You shouldn't have to do that. It's just not right."

Unprovoked attacks by loose dogs, he says, have long been a problem for guide dogs, and it is acute in David's area. But with limited means, and given the area's depressed housing market, moving to another neighborhood has not been an option. Sweet, brave, terrorized Isaac was finished as a guide dog after just five years. David recalls the deciding moment:

"I was walking him down the street, and this old lady was on the other side of the street with a little bitty dog on a leash and he tried to bolt after the dog. I knew it was over. I was working with John; we were constantly doing redirection retraining and trying to get him to not be aggressive when going by other dogs. But it was too late. We did everything we could. As long as we didn't encounter another dog, he was fine, he did his work well. But as soon as any dog came by, oh boy. The last time I took him to a convention, I couldn't go on an elevator with another guide dog. I didn't want to end up having him bite somebody else's dog. I didn't want to see him get put to sleep. So I called Fidelco and told them I'm not using the dog anymore, I just can't."

Isaac found a good home and a second career. A friend who was a case manager at the Harbor, a behavioral health care facility in Dade City that has placed foster children with David, was taking a similar job in Boston. The clinic she would be working at treats children who have been victims of sexual abuse. David says that the match was serendipitous, but perfect: "She said, 'I wish I had a dog like Isaac; the kids would talk to him all the time.' I said, 'He's retired—you can have him.' So he's in Boston now, working as a therapy dog. He just sits in her office all day. Kids come in and sit on him and roll all over him. He's got a good sweet life."

The parting was very sad, says David. This was the animal that gave him his life back. "But I was prepared for the change. You have to be, because you know that you're going to have to have another dog eventually. Honestly, I don't have time to grieve. And because I know where he is and what he's doing, I'm not unhappy. In fact, I'm grateful, because there's no way I could have kept him. If I had, he could have taught the new dog bad behavior with other dogs."

David is convinced that his crusades with Isaac have made Upton's job easier and ensured his safety. So far, the dog has suffered only one attack, right at the end of David's driveway, when a neighborhood pit bull dashed out suddenly, snarling, got the harness in her mouth, shook it violently back and forth, and would not let go. "Upton thought she was playing, so he was fine." David knew better, and over the noise, he yelled into his cell phone to summon police. This time, officers tracked down the owner, who had put the aggressive dog in his car and fled. David counts it as progress; the attacking dog has not troubled them since, and he gives its furious owner a wide berth.

David says, "For Isaac, I hate to say it—the attacks were anything but positive. But it did change the way that animal control, the sheriff's department, and EMS now handle people with service dogs."

Upton is at the door again at the sound of car doors in the driveway; Cristyn has arrived with her nine-month-old daughter, Kadin. They have barely crossed the threshold when the doting granddad has reached his arms out for the baby. Asked whether she and her sisters had been in favor of their father getting a guide dog, Cristyn lets out a hearty laugh.

"Are you kidding? I think we were happier than he was. We could stop being his guides and have a regular teenage life. Of course we love him like crazy. But it gets a little old, walking along that busy road in the baking sun, holding on to him. . . . Oh, we absolutely love the dog."

Upton is such a sweetheart that she would love to have him live with her family once he is retired from guide work. Malcolm, who has come in from school and sits curled next to David with his dog Maggie, cuts to the chase:

"I love Upton. And Maggie. I love my dad a lot. And I love that we can be normal together." He laughs. "Well, whatever normal is. Because of the dogs."

Despite his visual impairment, Malcolm is an enthusiastic and talented artist; a lot of his jeans and sweaters come from Goodwill, but somehow David always finds money for art supplies. And yes, Dad is strict. Yes, Upton is impossible to fool. But Malcolm figures that Dad must be doing something right, because all these foster kids keep coming back once they've been permanently placed or moved elsewhere in the system.

"We had fifteen staying here for Christmas," David says. "It was nuts, but kinda great."

He takes another slug of Diet Coke. To relax amid all the on-site therapy and tumult, he says he devours audiobooks; Braille is not an option because the stroke left him with neuropathy in his fingers. As Cristyn heads out to fetch an order of burgers for the boys' lunches, David says that the dog era has had another unforeseen benefit: physical fitness. "I was really fat. My kids couldn't put their arms around me. I got in shape because of all this walking with the dog. I love to walk, especially when it's cool. In the winter and fall we walk all the time. Spring, too."

In the hottest months, July through September, they walk at night when it's not beastly hot. And David is planning more adventurous walks with Upton. "My sister wants to do part of the Appalachian Trail and I want to go. There are parts that are not navigable even with a guide dog because there's too much climbing and too many rock formations. But I want to do the parts that I can."

He would also like to try skiing again. He won a trip to Aspen in February 2008 for selling the most raffle tickets on behalf of Challenge Aspen, a nonprofit organization that brings people with disabilities to Colorado to learn adaptive ways to ski, snowboard, fish, raft, and more—depending on the season. David would have had great difficulty claiming his prize, he says, if Fidelco trainers had not given Upton—about to be placed with him just after New Year's—some speedy additional training.

"They got me another dog really quickly because I was going

to Colorado and John wanted to make sure I had a dog before I went. I really didn't want to fly and navigate airports by myself. What's really weird is that John was training Upton in Boston when my friend Trish had just moved there with Isaac. So the dogs were both in Boston at the same time. They were training Upton on ice because the place I was going skiing has a lot of ice. They went out on a limb for me."

And it worked. In Colorado, David fell on ice a couple of times, but only when he was not with the dog—and no harm was suffered. On the slopes, Upton waited patiently as his new partner schussed out of sight. David navigated with the help of two ski buddies and a cane pole. His buddies called out the turns for him as he skimmed down the mountain with an unthinkable lightness of being. He says the experience afforded him one of the most astonishing, liberating moments he has enjoyed over these difficult last two decades.

It is nighttime on Highlands Mountain, but even David can discern, in the crisp white light of a full moon, that the trail crews have just finished their nightly grooming; sculpted by a bulldozer, the gleaming, high-contrast "corduroy" corrugations in the snow follow the curves and moguls. The guide dogs and visually impaired skiers—walking in boots now—climb slowly, steadily, behind their sighted guide partway up the slope. At the guide's signal, all unbuckle their dogs' harnesses and let them run free.

The dogs are heady with altitude, the sweet, frigid night air, and their sudden break from active duty. They are playing like puppies, wrestling, rolling in the snow, yipping and barking for the sheer joy of it. Holding their empty harnesses, their handlers marvel at the night, at the peace, the air, at their unspoken wonder at the day's glorious mobility. After a while, the guide signals that it's time to head back.

"Upton, come!"

The dog is there in a twinkling, shaking off snow and ready for the harness. David finishes buckling, takes the handle, and urges his partner forward. And carefully, confidently, man and shepherd walk down from the mountain.

EPILOGUE

Fifty years after the beginnings of their "breed within a breed" line in a small New England town, Fidelco guide dogs continue to make their quiet but deep impact on human lives. Occasionally, they make headlines:

LIGHTNING STRIKES BLIND MAN'S HOME; GUIDE DOG LEADS OWNER TO SAFETY

In July 2009, pretty, vigilant Unique, a female Fidelco shepherd, led eighty-three-year-old William Podolny to his front door and into the arms of firefighters in Manchester, Connecticut, when lightning ignited a blaze in his home. The raging fire took an hour and a half to contain, and destroyed the structure. The lightning had traveled down a propane line that led to a pair of five-hundred-gallon tanks. The dog did her job calmly and carefully amid the tumult of a still-raging thunderstorm and the shriek of smoke alarms.

Unique was on television for her dramatic rescue during a

storm cell that spawned two dozen 911 calls in ten minutes. But more often, public awareness of guide dogs' skills may turn on the small, unheralded moment. After all, restoring and maintaining the ability to lead a normal daily life may be a guide dog's greatest gift. Gail Gunn, who is currently partnered with her third Fidelco dog, Yankee, recalls an incident with her beloved first dog, Laurel: "I was at a restaurant. I was sitting on a tall stool in the bar area, and I dropped my credit card. I pointed to it and said, 'Laurel, fetch.' She picked it up neatly, right between her teeth, gave it to me, and lay back down. And all of a sudden I heard this applause. Half the restaurant had watched her."

Of course, the command "fetch" given to a guide dog involves an essential service, not a parlor trick. Visually impaired people partnered with guide dogs report any number of fascinating public perceptions overheard as they travel through life together:

"Hey, mister, izzat one of those blind dogs?"

"Mommy, look, it's a sightseeing dog!"

As guide dog users singly, persistently educate the rest of us on the wonders—and rights—of their canine partnerships, the virtues of patience and dedication and plenty of humor prevail in the busy kennels on those back acres of the Kaman Corporation. White Fidelco vans carrying dogs in training roll out early on weekday mornings for their appointed rounds in Windsor, Hartford, Boston, Manhattan, and countless challenging traffic sites in between. Fostered puppies continue to bounce out of station wagons for their required Saturday classes. The phone lines are always open to clients; guiding issues are routed to the training department. There are also health and injury queries, from a chewing habit to heat rash to a paw painfully snared in an escalator. And most often the response is "Let me put Robbie on the phone."

At the vortex of this busy enterprise, Robbie Kaman is a half-century's constant. Poring over breeders' magazines, keeping a watchful eye on the careers of littermates, she is still relying on good science and her ineffable "ear for the music" to improve her shepherds. Not long ago, Robbie commandeered the space for a small living area behind the kennels at Fidelco, anticipating a time when she may not commute here so easily from the estate she long shared with her husband. His ailments now require full-time care in a medical facility. She visits daily; he still likes to hear about the dogs and the students. Of their home, once bursting with pups, she now says, "It's too much house for me."

For the moment, her room at Fidelco is most often used by the women in the animal husbandry department who must monitor expectant breed dogs through many a long night. The Kamans have already deeded their twenty-two-acre estate to Fidelco, and when it is sold, Robbie will settle in at the place she loves best. She says her needs are simple, "just an efficiency apartment with a kitchenette, a little place to relax"—and a thirty-second commute to the dogs. She still has two dogs at home, one breeding female and another retired one, and they will move with her. At least that's the plan.

"If that doesn't work, I'll do something else. But most anytime, for as long as I can, this is where you'll find me. I wish people would quit asking me when I'm going to retire. It's not a job. It's what I do—period."

She says this is also true of the Kamans' old friend Karl Fuller, who is in his late eighties and still breeding and working the shepherds that produced the amazing Alma—she of the parking lot rescue so long ago. His grandson is currently running the sheep operation, and in the fall of 2009, the greatest honor was to be conferred on the master of Kirschental Kennels, the quiet shepherd whom dog people call "the iconic Karl Fuller." The

European herding competitions were to be held in his hometown of Stettbach, Germany, with considerable bark and pomp.

Wondering aloud whether she should get away after all these busy years and see their old friend honored, Robbie begins to describe these international herding dog trials. For dog people in thrall with a breed's peerless grace and dedication, the competition involves long days of eating dust and sidestepping sheep dung, and she just adores them.

"Oh, phooey. It's a bit hard to explain."

Robbie wonders whether human language can adequately describe the heart and soul of the working dog—the quiet but thrilling partnership that sent her out on the Kamans' own fields on crisp mornings with a dozen or so sheep and a German shepherd. With working guide dogs, the bond is more wondrous, more inspiring, and certainly more surprising to watch. And it is a big part of what draws her here every day.

Having rummaged in her office for a few moments, Robbie proffers a VHS tape labeled "Bundesleistungshuten, Obernau, 1987." German herding dog trials. "I probably sound a bit crazy trying to describe all this. So take a look," she says. "And understand what these animals do."

The tape is shot in grainy old video, overlaid with a wacky canned sound track that burbles a peppy instrumental version of the Everly Brothers' 1962 hit "Crying in the Rain" between barks and bleats. Yet it is indeed a very beautiful thing.

Bursting up from the rear of the herd, he is magnificent. The big male German shepherd has a smoky dark face and back, and a blaze of light fur on belly and legs, and for the duration of his trial, he is never still. The man, in traditional high boots, long coat, and a wide-brimmed hat, looks uncannily like the oil painting of Karl Fuller in Fidelco's lobby, tall, steely-gazed, and intent on his flock.

Fat-bottomed and bumptious, the sheep flood the narrow lane through the town, and the dog keeps them moving past distractions no Bavarian meadow normally affords: judges, spectators, camera-toting tourists, and a convoy of jouncing Audi sedans following the action toward a field.

Theirs is a seamless, wordless pas de deux—the man looking only rarely at the dog, speaking to him with a glance, a barely perceptible hand signal, a slight wave of his crook. Never, not for a second, does the dog stop moving, tail down, ears flat, as he snaps a bleating stray back into the big, woolly amoeba he is moving toward a distant pen. Suddenly, the dog dives low, disappears into the herd to turn it, and reemerges through the dust. His eyes are searching the man's back for a signal—a raised finger, the drop of a shoulder.

Now the screen is an Impressionist scrim of blurry wool, light, and dust; moving behind it all, only a pair of black pointed ears are visible bouncing above the sheep's backs as the dog neatens up the perimeter.

His perfect dance is spellbinding in its fierce concentration, so fluid yet punctuated by sidelong runs in ever-decreasing arcs, by quick pirouettes and powerful bursts of speed. The man walks at the head of the flock, still stone-faced beneath his hat brim, and stands by the fence as the sheep pour into the pen. When they have all passed through, he draws railings across the opening to close the sheep in. And only then does the panting dog lie down.

The man doffs his shepherd's hat to the loudly appreciative crowd. A fleeting and very knowing look passes between him and the dog. They walk off slowly, side by side.

DO YOU KNOW SOMEONE WHO
IS LOSING HIS OR HER VISION?

Many organizations are dedicated to helping men and women who are visually impaired. There are many devices available to help those with low vision utilize what they have and training classes are also available. To learn about services in your area, contact your state agency for the blind. They can provide counseling and referral services that are the most appropriate.